Con

Atlantic
Canada
BIRDS

Contributors:

Roger Burrows, Krista Kagume & Carmen Adams

Lone Pine Publishing

© 2005 by Lone Pine Publishing
First printed in 2005   10 9 8 7 6 5 4 3
Printed in China

The Publisher: Lone Pine Publishing
10145 – 81 Avenue
Edmonton, AB T6E 1W9

Website: www.lonepinepublishing.com

Library and Archives Canada Cataloguing in Publication

   Compact guide to the birds of Atlantic Canada / contributors, Roger Burrows ... [et al.].

   Includes bibliographical references and index.
   ISBN-13: 978-1-55105-473-5. ISBN-10: 1-55105-473-6

   1. Birds—Atlantic Provinces—Identification. I. Burrows, Roger, 1942–

QL685.5.A9C64 2005   598'.09715   C2004-907292-7

Editorial Director: Nancy Foulds
Project Editor: Genevieve Boyer
Production Manager: Gene Longson
Book Design: Curt Pillipow
Cover Design: Gerry Dotto
Cover Illustration: Gary Ross
Illustrations: Gary Ross, Ted Nordhagen, Ewa Pluciennik
Egg Photography: Alan Bibby
Layout & Production: Elliot Engley
Scanning & Digital Film: Elite Lithographers Co.

We acknowledge the financial support of the Government of Canada through the Book Publishing Industry Development Program (BPIDP) for our publishing activities.

PC: 13

Contents

WATERFOWL

Canada Goose
size 89 cm • p. 18

Blue-winged Teal
size 39 cm • p. 20

Common Eider
size 63 cm • p. 22

White-winged Scoter
size 55 cm • p. 24

Bufflehead
size 36 cm • p. 26

Common Merganser
size 63 cm • p. 28

GROUSE

Ruffed Grouse
size 43 cm • p. 30

Common Loon
size 80 cm • p. 32

Sooty Shearwater
size 44 cm • p. 34

DIVING BIRDS

Leach's Storm-Petrel
size 21 cm • p. 36

Northern Gannet
size 94 cm • p. 38

Double-crested Cormorant
size 74 cm • p. 40

BITTERNS, HERONS & VULTURES

American Bittern
size 64 cm • p. 42

Great Blue Heron
size 135 cm • p. 44

Turkey Vulture
size 74 cm • p. 46

BIRDS OF PREY

Osprey
size 60 cm • p. 48

Bald Eagle
size 93 cm • p. 50

Northern Harrier
size 51 cm • p. 52

Sharp-shinned Hawk
size 31 cm • p. 54

Red-tailed Hawk
size 55 cm • p. 56

Peregrine Falcon
size 43 cm • p. 58

Sora
size 23 cm • p. 60

Killdeer
size 26 cm • p. 62

Spotted Sandpiper
size 19 cm • p. 64

Sanderling
size 20 cm • p. 66

Wilson's Snipe
size 28 cm • p. 68

Red-necked Phalarope
size 22 cm • p. 70

Bonaparte's Gull
size 33 cm • p. 72

Herring Gull
size 62 cm • p. 74

Great Black-backed Gull
size 76 cm • p. 76

Common Tern
size 37 cm • p. 78

Common Murre
size 43 cm • p. 80

Black Guillemot
size 33 cm • p. 82

Atlantic Puffin
size 32 cm • p. 84

Rock Pigeon
size 32 cm • p. 86

Mourning Dove
size 31 cm • p. 88

OWLS

Great Horned Owl
size 55 cm • p. 90

Snowy Owl
size 60 cm • p. 92

Common Nighthawk
size 24 cm • p. 94

NIGHTHAWKS, SWIFTS & HUMMINGBIRDS

Chimney Swift
size 13 cm • p. 96

Ruby-throated Hummingbird
size 9 cm • p. 98

Belted Kingfisher
size 32 cm • p. 100

WOODPECKERS & FLICKERS

Yellow-bellied Sapsucker
size 19 cm • p. 102

Downy Woodpecker
size 17 cm • p. 104

Northern Flicker
size 33 cm • p. 106

FLYCATCHERS & KINGBIRDS

Pileated Woodpecker
size 45 cm • p. 108

Olive-sided Flycatcher
size 19 cm • p. 110

Eastern Kingbird
size 22 cm • p. 112

SHRIKES & VIREOS

Northern Shrike
size 25 cm • p. 114

Red-eyed Vireo
size 15 cm • p. 116

Gray Jay
size 31 cm • p. 118

JAYS, CROWS & RAVENS

Blue Jay
size 30 cm • p. 120

American Crow
size 48 cm • p. 122

Common Raven
size 61 cm • p. 124

Horned Lark
size 18 cm • p. 126

Tree Swallow
size 14 cm • p. 128

Barn Swallow
size 18 cm • p. 130

LARKS & SWALLOWS

Black-capped Chickadee
size 14 cm • p. 132

Red-breasted Nuthatch
size 11 cm • p. 134

Brown Creeper
size 13 cm • p. 136

CHICKADEES, WRENS & NUTHATCHES

Winter Wren
size 10 cm • p. 138

Golden-crowned Kinglet
size 10 cm • p. 140

Swainson's Thrush
size 18 cm • p. 142

KINGLETS & THRUSHES

American Robin
size 25 cm • p. 144

Gray Catbird
size 23 cm • p. 146

European Starling
size 22 cm • p. 148

MIMICS, STARLINGS & WAXWINGS

Cedar Waxwing
size 18 cm • p. 150

Yellow Warbler
size 13 cm • p. 152

American Redstart
size 13 cm • p. 154

WOOD-WARBLERS & TANAGERS

Ovenbird
size 15 cm • p. 156

Scarlet Tanager
size 18 cm • p. 158

Chipping Sparrow
size 14 cm • p. 160

SPARROWS

SPARROWS, GROSBEAKS & BUNTINGS

Song Sparrow
size 16 cm • p. 162

Dark-eyed Junco
size 16 cm • p. 164

Rose-breasted Grosbeak
size 20 cm • p. 166

Indigo Bunting
size 14 cm • p. 168

Red-winged Blackbird
size 21 cm • p. 170

Eastern Meadowlark
size 24 cm • p. 172

BLACKBIRDS & ALLIES

Brown-headed Cowbird
size 17 cm • p. 174

White-winged Crossbill
size 16 cm • p. 176

Common Redpoll
size 13 cm • p. 178

FINCHLIKE BIRDS

American Goldfinch
size 13 cm • p. 180

House Sparrow
size 16 cm • p. 182

Introduction

If you have ever admired a songbird's pleasant notes, been fascinated by a diving seabird or wondered how woodpeckers keep sawdust out of their nostrils, this book is for you. There is so much to discover about birds and their surroundings that birding is becoming one of the fastest growing hobbies on the planet. Many people find it relaxing, while others enjoy its outdoor appeal. Some people see it as a way to reconnect with nature, an opportunity to socialize with like-minded people or a way to monitor the environment.

Whether you are just beginning to take an interest in birds or you can already identify many species, there is always more to learn. We've highlighted both the remarkable traits and the more typical behaviours displayed by some of Atlantic Canada's most abundant or noteworthy birds. A few live in specialized habitats, but most are common species that you have a good chance of encountering on most outings or in your backyard.

BIRDING IN ATLANTIC CANADA

More than 320 bird species are found in Atlantic Canada on a regular basis, largely because of the geographical and biological diversity of the area. The Atlantic provinces offer a variety of unsurpassed bird-watching opportunities. Some of the largest Common Murre breeding colonies are found off the rocky coasts, brilliant Scarlet Tanangers sing in the forests and cormorants perch on piers to dry their wings. Some of our birds, such as the Atlantic Puffin, are

Common Murre

found nowhere else in Canada. Our coastlines draw nesting pelagic birds during summer, and waterfowl, geese, loons and grebes during winter. Many of Atlantic Canada's birds are year-round residents, whereas others visit our area to breed, or pass through on annual migrations.

Scarlet Tanager

Identifying birds in action and under varying conditions involves skill, timing and luck. The more you know about a bird—its range, preferred habitat, food preferences and hours and seasons of activity—the better your chances will be of seeing it. Generally, spring and autumn are the busiest birding times. Temperatures are moderate then, many species of birds are on the move, and male songbirds are belting out their unique courtship songs. Birds are usually most active in the early morning hours, except in winter when they forage during the day while temperatures are milder.

Another useful clue for correctly recognizing birds is knowledge of their habitat. Simply put, a bird's habitat is the place where it normally lives. Some birds prefer open water, some birds are found in cattail marshes, others like mature coniferous forest, and still others prefer abandoned agricultural fields overgrown with tall grass

Atlantic Puffin

and shrubs. Habitats are just like neighbourhoods: if you associate friends with the suburb in which they live, you can easily learn to associate specific birds with their preferred habitats. Only in migration, especially during inclement weather, do some birds leave their usual habitat.

Bonaparte's Gull

Atlantic Canada has a long tradition of friendly, recreational birding. In general, birders in the Atlantic provinces are willing to help beginners, share their knowledge and involve novices in their projects. Christmas bird counts, breeding bird surveys, nest box programs, migration monitoring and birding lectures and workshops provide a chance for birdwatchers of all levels to interact and share the splendour of birds. Bird hotlines in Atlantic Canada provide up-to-date information on the sightings of rarities, which are often easier to relocate than you might think. The following is a brief list of contacts that will help you get involved:

Nature NB
924 Prospect Street, Suite 110
Fredericton, NB
E3B 2T9
http://www.naturenb.ca

Nature Nova Scotia
Nova Scotia Museum
1747 Summer Street
Halifax, NS
B3H 3A6
http://www.naturens.ca

Natural History Society of PEI
PO Box 2346
Charlottetown, PEI
C1A 8C1
http://www.gov.pe.ca/infopei/index.php3?number=2388

Natural History Society of Newfoundland and Labrador
PO Box 1013
St. John's, NL
A1C 5M3
http://www.nhs.nf.ca/

Club des Ornithologues de la Gaspésie
428, boulevard Pabos
Pabos, QC
G0C 2H0
http://www.cogaspesie.org/

BIRD HOTLINES
New Brunswick (506) 384-6397
Nova Scotia (902) 852-2428

BIRD FEEDING
Many people set up bird feeders in their backyard, especially in winter. It is possible to attract specific birds by choosing the right kind of food and style of feeder. Keep your feeder stocked through late spring, because birds have a hard time finding food before the flowers bloom,

*Black-capped
Chickadee*

seeds develop and insects hatch. Contrary to popular opinion, birds do not become dependent on feeders, nor do they subsequently forget to forage naturally. Be sure to clean your feeder and the surrounding area regularly to prevent the spread of disease.

Landscaping your property with native plants is another way of providing natural foods for birds.

Sharp-shinned Hawk

Flocks of waxwings have a keen eye for red mountain ash berries and hummingbirds enjoy columbine flowers. The cumulative effects of "nature-scaping" urban yards can be a significant step toward habitat conservation (especially when you consider that habitat is often lost in small amounts—a seismic line is cut in one area and a highway is built in another). Many good books and web sites about attracting wildlife to your backyard are available.

ATLANTIC CANADA'S TOP BIRDING SITES

The Atlantic provinces are as diverse as they are distinct, with salty lagoons, rolling dunes and the vast coniferous forests. Atlantic Canada can be divided into three natural regions: Boreal Forest, Great Lakes–St. Lawrence Forest and Acadian Forest. Each region is composed of a number of different habitats and contains a wealth of wildlife.

There are hundreds of good birding areas throughout Atlantic Canada. The following sites have been selected to represent a broad range of bird communities and habitats, with an emphasis on accessibility.

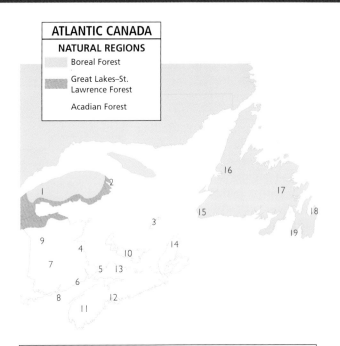

| ATLANTIC CANADA |
| NATURAL REGIONS |
| Boreal Forest |
| Great Lakes–St. Lawrence Forest |
| Acadian Forest |

Maritime Quebec
1. Rimouski
2. Forillon National Park
3. Îles de la Madeleine

New Brunswick
4. Kouchibouguac National Park
5. Cape Jourimain
6. Fundy National Park
7. Odell Park, Fredericton
8. Grand Manan Island
9. Plaster Rock–Nictau

Prince Edward Island
10. Brackley–Covehead Marshes

Nova Scotia
11. Kejimkujik National Park
12. Point Pleasant Park, Halifax
13. Wallace Bay
14. Cape Breton Highlands National Park

Newfoundland
15. Codroy Valley
16. Gros Morne National Park
17. Terra Nova National Park
18. St. John's Metropolitan Area
19. Cape St. Mary's

ABOUT THE SPECIES ACCOUNTS

This book gives detailed accounts of 83 species of birds that can be expected in Atlantic Canada on an annual basis. The order of the birds and their common and scientific names follow the American Ornithologists' Union's *Check-list of North American Birds* (7th edition, July 1998, and its supplements).

As well as showing the identifying features of the bird, each species account also attempts to bring the bird to life by describing its various character traits. One of the challenges of birding is that many species look different in spring and summer than they do in autumn and winter. Many birds have breeding and nonbreeding plumages, and immature birds often look different from their parents. This book does not try to describe or illustrate all the different plumages of a species; instead, it tries to focus on the forms that are most likely to be seen in our area.

Great Blue Heron

Other ID: Large illustrations point out prominent field marks that will help you tell each bird apart. The descriptions favour easily understood language instead of technical terms. Some of the most common anatomical features of birds are pointed out in the Glossary illustration (p. 184).

Size: The average length of the bird's body from bill to tail, as well as wingspan, are given and are approximate measurements of the bird as it is seen in nature. The size is sometimes given as a range, because there is variation between individuals, or between males and females.

Voice: You will hear many birds, particularly songbirds, which may remain hidden from view. Memorable paraphrases of distinctive sounds will aid you in identifying a species by ear.

Status: A general comment, such as "common," "uncommon" or "rare," is usually sufficient to describe the relative abundance of a species. Situations are bound to vary somewhat since migratory pulses, seasonal changes and centres of activity tend to concentrate or disperse birds.

Habitat: The habitats listed describe where each species is most commonly found. Because of the freedom flight gives them, birds can turn up in almost any type of habitat. However, they will usually be found in environments that provide the specific food, water, cover and, in some cases, nesting habitat that they need to survive.

Ruffed Grouse

Range Maps: The range map for each species shows the overall range of the species in an average year. Most birds will confine their annual movements to this range, although each year some birds wander beyond their traditional boundaries. The maps show breeding, summer and winter ranges, as well as migratory pathways—areas of the region where birds may appear while en route to nesting or winter habitat. The representations of the pathways do not distinguish high-use migration corridors from areas that are seldom used.

Range Map Symbols

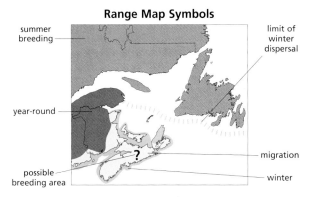

summer breeding

limit of winter dispersal

year-round

possible breeding area

migration

winter

Similar Birds: Easily confused species are illustrated for each account; sometimes accidental or rarely seen similar birds are shown. If you concentrate on the most relevant field marks, the subtle differences between species can be reduced to easily identifiable traits.

Nesting: In each species account, nest location and structure, clutch size, incubation period and parental duties are discussed. A photo of the bird's egg is also provided. The nesting behaviour of birds that do not nest in our region is not described. Remember that birding ethics discourage the disturbance of active bird nests. If you disturb a nest, you may drive off the parents during a critical period or expose defenceless young to predators.

Canada Goose
Branta canadensis

Canada Geese mate for life and are devoted parents. The young remain with their parents for nearly a year, which increases their chance of survival. • Rescuers who care for injured geese report that these birds readily adopt their human caregivers. However, wild geese can be aggressive, especially when defending young or competing for food. Hissing sounds and low, outstretched necks are signs that you should give these birds some space. • Geese graze on aquatic grasses and sprouts, and they also tip up to grab aquatic roots and tubers.

Other ID: light brown underparts; dark brown upperparts. *In flight:* flocks fly in V-formation.
Size: *L* 92–122 cm; *W* up to 1.8 m.
Voice: loud, familiar *ah-honk*.
Status: common to locally abundant migrant; uncommon to locally abundant winter resident; uncommon breeder.
Habitat: lakeshores, riverbanks, ponds, farmlands and city parks.

Similar Birds

Brant

Greater White-fronted Goose

Snow Goose

long, black neck

white "chin strap"

short, black tail

Nesting: usually on the ground; female builds a nest of grass and mud, lined with down; white eggs are 87 x 58 mm; female incubates 3–8 eggs for 25–28 days; goslings are born in May.

Did You Know?

A migrating Canada Goose will occasionally allow a smaller bird to hitch a ride on its back!

Look For

Several subspecies, each with unique features and varying size, can be found across Atlantic Canada.

Blue-winged Teal
Anas discors

Blue-winged Teals and other dabbling ducks feed by tipping up their tails and dunking their heads underwater. "Dabblers" have small feet situated near the centre of their bodies. Other ducks, such as scaups, scoters and Buffleheads, dive underwater to feed, propelled by large feet set farther back on their bodies.

• The scientific name *discors* is Latin for "without harmony," which might refer to this bird's call as it takes flight.

Other ID: broad, flat bill. *Male:* white undertail coverts. *Female:* mottled brown overall. *In flight:* blue forewing patch; green speculum.
Size: L 36–41 cm; W 58 cm.
Voice: *Male:* soft *keck-keck-keck*. *Female:* soft quacks.
Status: fairly common to common migrant; rare to uncommon breeder; a few may overwinter.
Habitat: shallow lake edges and wetlands; prefers areas with short but dense emergent vegetation.

Similar Birds

Green-winged Teal

Northern Shoveler

white throat

blue grey head

black-spotted
breast and sides

♀

♂

white crescent
on face

Nesting: along a grassy shoreline or in a meadow; nest is built with grass and considerable amounts of down; cream-coloured eggs are 46 x 32 mm; female incubates 8–13 eggs for 23–27 days.

Did You Know?

Blue-winged Teals summer as far north as the Canadian tundra and overwinter mainly in Central and South America.

Look For

Small, speedy Blue-winged Teals are renowned for their aviation skills. They can be identified by their small size and by the sharp twists and turns they execute in flight.

Common Eider
Somateria mollissima

This stocky, solid-looking bird is equipped with a
high metabolic rate, insulative "eider down" and a
feathered bill, almost to the nostril, to survive the
unpredictable, frigid waves off the Atlantic Coast.
It is almost entirely marine, only occasionally visiting freshwater lakes. • The Common Eider is a
deep-sea diver, travelling sometimes more than
45 metres underwater to dine on molluscs.
The aquatic invertebrates are pried free of
their benthic footholds and swallowed
whole, then crushed in the gizzard of the
Common Eider.

Other ID: *Male:* black and white overall. *Female:*
grey to rusty brown overall.
Size: L 58–68 cm; W 88–106 cm.
Voice: *Male:* raucous, moaning *he-ho-ha-ho* or
a-o-waa-a-o-waa; ah-oo and *k'doo* courtship calls.
Female: Mallard-like *wak-wak-wak-wak-
wak;* courtship call is *aw-aw-aw.*
Status: locally abundant winter resident;
locally common breeder.
Habitat: shallow coastal waters in all
seasons; occasionally seen on large freshwater lakes. *Breeding:* rocky shorelines,
islands or tundra close to water.

Similar Birds

King Eider   Surf Scoter   White-winged Scoter (p. 24)

smoothly sloping forehead

grey bill and nasal shield

pale green nasal shield and nape

barred breast, flanks and back

Nesting: colonial; in a shallow depression on a rocky shelf; nest is lined with down and plant material; olive grey eggs are 77 x 52 mm; female incubates 3–6 eggs for 24–25 days.

Did You Know?

During the breeding season, female eiders pluck downy feathers from their own bodies to provide insulation and camouflage for their eggs.

Look For

In flight, the Common Eider flies close to the water's surface with its head lowered, and its noteworthy wingspan is comparable to that of a hawk.

White-winged Scoter
Melanitta fusca

The largest of the three North American scoter species, the White-winged Scoter shares the same stocky, dark body as the Surf Scoter but lacks the white forehead and nape. Furthermore, the White-wing doesn't limit its travels to North America; it breeds throughout America, Europe and Asia.

• Scoters have small wings relative to the weight of their bodies and require a long stretch of water for takeoff. The easiest time to identify this bird is when it takes flight—look for a flash of its white inner wing patches contrasted against its otherwise dark black plumage.

Other ID: *Female:* brownish grey plumage and bill; 2 large, indistinct pale patches on side of head. *In flight:* conspicuous white area on hindwing.
Size: *L* 48–61 cm; *W* 87 cm.
Voice: courting pair produces guttural and harsh noises, between a *crook* and a quack.
Status: common year-round.
Habitat: *Breeding:* lakes, muskeg wetlands and slow-flowing rivers. *Winter:* coastal bays and estuaries.

Similar Birds

Surf Scoter

Black Scoter

American Coot

orange to yellowish
tip of bill

pale eye
surrounded by
white crescent

♂

bulbous bill with
feathering

Nesting: nesting not confirmed in Atlantic Canada; among bushes near shorelines; in a shallow scrape lined with sticks, leaves, grass and down; creamy to buff eggs are 67 x 46 mm; female incubates 9–14 eggs for up to 28 days.

Did You Know?

The name "scoter" may be derived from the way this bird scoots across the water's surface from one foraging site to another.

Look For

When diving for food, the bulky body of this bird, combined with the edge of its leading wing hitting the water, creates a splash almost a metre high.

Bufflehead

Bucephala albeola

The tiny Bufflehead might be the first diving duck you learn to identify. With its simple, bold plumage, this abundant duck resembles few other species. The striking white patch on the rear of the male's head stands out, even from a distance.
• Buffleheads often nest in tree cavities, using abandoned woodpecker nests or natural holes. After hatching, the ducklings remain in the nest chamber for up to three days before jumping out and tumbling to the ground.

Other ID: short, grey bill; short neck.
Male: dark back; white neck and underparts.
Female: dark brown head and upperparts; light brown sides. *In flight:* white speculum.
Size: *L* 33–38 cm; *W* 53 cm.
Voice: *Male:* growling call. *Female:* harsh quack.
Status: common to locally abundant in migration and winter; rare at other times.
Habitat: open water of lakes, large ponds and rivers; coastal bays and estuaries.

Similar Birds

Hooded Merganser

Barrow's Goldeneye

Common Goldeneye

white, oval ear patch

iridescent, dark green or purple head usually appears black

white wedge on back of head

Nesting: does not nest in Atlantic Canada; nest is in a tree cavity; may be unlined or down-filled; creamy or buff eggs are 50 x 36 mm; female incubates 6–12 eggs for 28–33 days.

Did You Know?

Unlike other diving ducks, Buffleheads can take off straight from the water, without a running start.

Look For

Buffleheads gather where tidal bays are constricted. They spend as much time chasing each other as they do diving for molluscs such as snails.

Common Merganser
Mergus merganser

Lumbering like a jumbo jet, the Common Merganser must run along the surface of the water, beating its heavy wings to gain sufficient lift to take off. Once up and away, this large duck flies arrow-straight and low over the water, making broad, sweeping turns to follow the meandering shore-lines of rivers and lakes. • Common Mergansers are highly social and often gather in large groups during migration. In winter, any source of open water with a fish-filled shoal will support good numbers of these skilled divers.

Other ID: large, elongated body. *Male:* white body plumage; black stripe on back; dark eyes. *Female:* grey body; orangy eyes.
Size: L 56–69 cm; W 86 cm.
Voice: *Male:* harsh *uig-a*, like a guitar twang. *Female:* harsh *karr karr*.
Status: uncommon to common in migration and winter; rare to common breeder.
Habitat: large rivers and deep lakes; also coastal bays and estuaries in winter.

Similar Birds

Red-breasted Merganser

Northern Shoveler

Common Loon (p. 32)

glossy, green head without crest

blood red bill and feet

rusty neck and crested head

orange bill

clean white "chin" and breast

Nesting: in a tree cavity; occasionally on the ground, on a cliff ledge or in a large nest box; usually close to water; pale buff eggs are 66 x 46 mm; female incubates 8–11 eggs for 30–35 days.

Did You Know?

The Common Merganser is the most widespread and abundant merganser in North America. It also occurs in Europe and Asia.

Look For

In flight, this duck has shallow wingbeats and an arrowlike, compressed body.

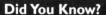

Ruffed Grouse
Bonasa umbellus

If you hear a loud booming that echoes through
the forest, you are likely listening to a male Ruffed
Grouse "drumming" to announce his territory.
Every spring, and occasionally in autumn, the male
grouse struts along a fallen log with his tail fanned
and his neck feathers ruffed, beating
the air periodically with accelerating
wingstrokes. • In winter, scales grow out
along the sides of the Ruffed Grouse's feet,
creating temporary "snowshoes." Though many
birds can walk on snow, only grouse and ptarmigan have this special feature.

Other ID: mottled, grey brown overall.
Female: incomplete subterminal tail band.
Size: L 38–48 cm; W 56 cm.
Voice: *Male:* hollow, drumming courtship
display of accelerating, deep booms.
Female: clucks and "hisses" around her
chicks.
Status: common year-round resident.
Habitat: deciduous and mixed forests
and riparian woodlands; favours young,
second-growth stands with birch and
poplar.

Similar Birds

Spruce Grouse

Sharp-tailed Grouse

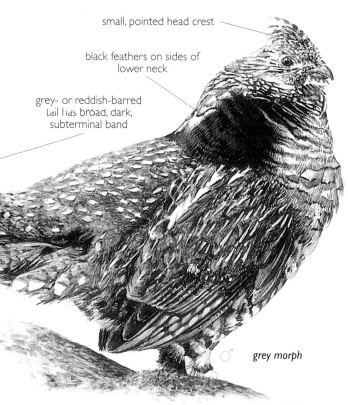

small, pointed head crest

black feathers on sides of lower neck

grey- or reddish-barred tail has broad, dark, subterminal band

♂ *grey morph*

Nesting: in a shallow depression among leaf litter; buff-coloured eggs are 40 x 30 mm; female incubates 9–12 eggs for 23–25 days.

Did You Know?

During winter, Ruffed Grouse bury themselves in snowbanks to keep warm.

Look For

When a potential threat approaches, a Ruffed Grouse will often freeze to camouflage itself against the forest floor. For every grouse seen, many more go unnoticed.

Common Loon

annapolis Royal

Gavia immer

When the haunting call of the Common Loon pierces a still evening, cottagers know that summer has begun. Loons actually have several different calls. Frightened loons give a "laughing" distress call; separated pairs seem to wail *where aaare you?* and groups give soft, cohesive hoots as they fly.
• Common Loons are well suited to their aquatic lifestyle. Most birds have hollow bones, but loons have solid bones that reduce their buoyancy and make it easier for them to dive.

Other ID: *Breeding:* stout, thick, black bill; white breast and underparts. *Nonbreeding:* much duller plumage; sandy brown back; light underparts. *In flight:* long wings beat constantly; hunchbacked appearance; legs trail behind tail.
Size: *L* 71–89 cm; *W* 1.2–1.5 m.
Voice: alarm call is a quavering tremolo; also wails, hoots and yodels.
Status: common migrant and winter resident; fairly common breeder.
Habitat: large lakes and rivers, often with islands that provide undisturbed shorelines for nesting. *In migration* and *winter:* saltwater bays and headlands.

Similar Birds

Red-throated Loon

Red-breasted Merganser

Common Merganser (p. 28)

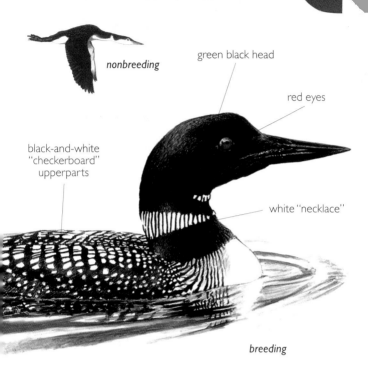

nonbreeding

green black head

red eyes

black-and-white "checkerboard" upperparts

white "necklace"

breeding

Nesting: nest is a mound of aquatic vegetation; darkly spotted, olive brown eggs are 90 x 57 mm; both parents incubate 1–3 eggs for 24–31 days.

Did You Know?

Hungry loons will chase fish to depths of 55 metres—as deep as an Olympic-sized swimming pool is long.

Look For

Rear-placed legs make walking on land awkward for these birds. The word "loon" is probably derived from the Scandinavian word *lom,* which means "clumsy person."

Sooty Shearwater
Puffinus griseus

You may spot this bird without even venturing out to sea. The Sooty Shearwater is one of the world's most common birds and is one of the few shearwater species that can be spotted in the waters below the surf line, where it feeds on large concentrations of schooling fish. • When our summer draws to an end, Sooty Shearwaters chase the sun back to their breeding grounds on islands in the Southern Hemisphere. • The Sooty Shearwater shares many features with the Northern Fulmar but has a long, slender, black bill. It is called "Black Hag" by resident fishermen.

Other ID: *In flight:* silvery streak on underwing linings.
Size: *L* 41–46 cm; *W* 1.0 m.
Voice: generally silent; occasionally utters quarrelsome calls when competing for food.
Status: common to abundant visitor in migration and summer; otherwise rare.
Habitat: open ocean; concentrates at upwellings and current edges along the continental shelf.

Similar Birds

Northern Fulmar

Greater Shearwater

Pomarine Jaeger

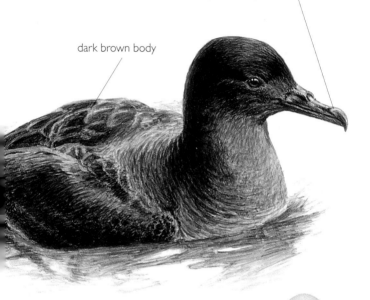

slender, black bill
with small "tube" on
upper mandible

dark brown body

Nesting: does not nest in Atlantic Canada;
breeds on islands in the Southern Hemisphere;
nest burrow is lined with leaves and grass; white
eggs are 60 x 40 mm; pair incubates 1 egg for
52–56 days.

Did You Know?

Albatrosses, shearwaters
and storm-petrels have a
keen sense of smell that
helps them to locate
food, breeding sites and
other individuals.

Look For

The Sooty Shearwater glides
on its long, pointed wings,
flapping intermittently with
rapid, deep wingbeats.

Sept. 1/16 *annapolis*
Royal

Leach's Storm-Petrel

Oceanodroma leucorhoa

These mysterious birds are like nighthawks, with deep wingbeats and gliding flight. Mariners believed that the presence of these "Sea Swallows" was a sign of an approaching storm. They were probably right—the Leach's Storm-Petrel is often caught up in storms and forced inshore, and occasionally inland, where their inability to take off from level ground renders them helpless. • The Leach's Storm-Petrel is seldom seen carrying out its parental duties at night—its young are concealed in underground burrows.

Other ID: dark brown overall; slender, black bill; black legs.
Size: *L* 20–23 cm; *W* 51 cm.
Voice: commonly gives purring, chattering and trilling nocturnal notes at the nest site; otherwise usually silent.
Status: locally abundant breeder and summer visitor; uncommon to common migrant.
Habitat: usually in warmer waters at least 120 km from shore.

Similar Birds

Wilson's Storm-Petrel

Sooty Shearwater (p. 34)

light, diagonal band on
dark upperwings

whitish rump with
grey centre line

Nesting: colonial; on an offshore island or islet;
uses a rock crevice or an old burrow, or male
excavates a burrow; white egg is 33 x 24 mm;
pair incubates 1 egg for 37–50 days.

Did You Know?

The female Leach's
Storm-Petrel possesses a
sperm-storage gland that
allows for the pair to be
separated prior to egg
laying.

Look For

These birds occasionally
hang motionless in the air
with their wings raised
slightly and their feet patter-
ing on the water's surface.

Northern Gannet
Morus bassanus

The Northern Gannet, with its elegant face "mask" and high forehead, slices through the open ocean air with blackened wing tips. This gentle-looking bird does not breed until it is at least five years of age and mates for life. Pairs affectionately dip their bills to the breast of their mate, bowing, raising their wings and preening each other to reestablish their bond each year. But, when it is time for dinner, the Northern Gannet has no mercy for schooling herring and mackerel.

black wing tips

Other ID: white overall; long narrow wings; pointed tail; black feet.
Size: L 89–97 cm; W 1.8 m.
Voice: usually silent at sea; feeding flocks may exchange grating growls.
Status: locally common breeder; common offshore in migration; uncommon offshore in winter.
Habitat: roosts and feeds in open ocean waters most of the year; often seen well offshore; regularly seen inshore during migration.

Similar Birds

Snow Goose

In summer, gannets briefly seek land for nesting. Look for them at Bird Rocks on Îles de la Madeleine and Cape St. Mary's on the island of Newfoundland.

buffy wash
on nape

thick,
tapered, pale
grey bill

Nesting: on protected mainland or island sea cliffs; male builds nest of seaweed, vegetation, dirt and feathers glued together with droppings; pale blue to white egg is 82 x 49 mm; pair incubates 1 egg for 43–45 days.

Did You Know?

Squadrons of gannets soaring at heights of more than 30 metres above the water will suddenly arrest their flight by folding their wings back, then they simultaneously plunge headfirst into the ocean depths in pursuit of schooling fish.

annapolis Royal, N.S.

Double-crested Cormorant
Phalacrocorax auritus

The Double-crested Cormorant looks like a bird but smells and swims like a fish. With a long, rudderlike tail and excellent underwater vision, this slick-feathered bird has mastered the underwater world. Most water birds have waterproof feathers, but the structure of this bird's feathers allows water in. "Wettable" feathers make this bird less buoyant, which in turn makes it a better diver. The Double-crested Cormorant also has sealed nostrils for diving, and therefore must fly with its bill slightly open.

Other ID: all-black body; blue eyes. *Immature:* brown upperparts; buff throat and breast; yellowish throat patch. *In flight:* rapid wingbeats; kinked neck.
Size: *L* 66–81 cm; *W* 1.3 m.
Voice: generally quiet; may issue piglike grunts or croaks, especially near nest colonies.
Status: uncommon to locally common migrant and breeder; rare in winter.
Habitat: large lakes and large, meandering rivers.

Similar Birds

Great Cormorant   Common Loon (p. 32)

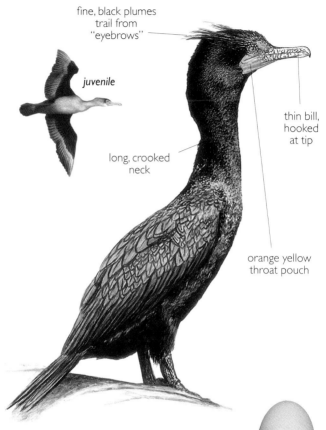

fine, black plumes trail from "eyebrows"

juvenile

thin bill, hooked at tip

long, crooked neck

orange yellow throat pouch

Nesting: colonial; on an island or high in a tree; platform nest is made of sticks and guano; bluish white eggs are 51 x 38 mm; both sexes incubate 2–7 eggs for 25–30 days.

Did You Know?

Japanese fishermen sometimes use cormorants on leashes to catch fish. This traditional method of fishing is called *ukai*.

Look For

Double-crested Cormorants often perch on trees or piers with their wings partially spread. Lacking oil glands, they use the wind to dry their feathers.

American Bittern
Botaurus lentiginosus

The American Bittern's deep, pumping call is as common in a spring marsh as the sound of croaking frogs, but this well-camouflaged bird remains well hidden. When an intruder approaches, the bittern freezes with its bill pointed skyward—its vertically streaked, brown plumage blends perfectly with the surrounding marsh. In most cases, intruders simply pass by without ever noticing the bird. An American Bittern will adopt this reedlike position even in an open field, apparently unaware that a lack of cover betrays its presence!

Other ID: brown upperparts; rich buff flanks and sides; white underparts; yellow legs and feet; black outer wings; short tail.
Size: *L* 59–69 cm; *W* 1.1 m.
Voice: deep, slow, resonant, repetitive *pomp-er-lunk* or *onk-a-BLONK;* most often heard in the evening or at night.
Status: rare to fairly common migrant and breeder; very rare in winter.
Habitat: marshes, wetlands and lake edges with tall, dense grasses, sedges, bulrushes and cattails.

Similar Birds

Least Bittern

Look For

This bird patiently stands and waits for prey to come within its reach. It may sway its head as it waits, mimicking the movement of surrounding vegetation.

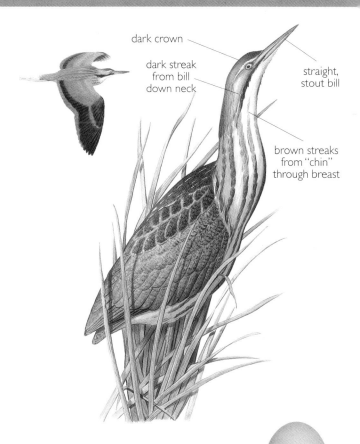

dark crown

dark streak
from bill
down neck

straight,
stout bill

brown streaks
from "chin"
through breast

Nesting: above the waterline in dense vegetation; platform nest is made of sedges and reeds; pale olive or buff eggs are 49 x 37 mm; female incubates 3–5 eggs for 24–28 days.

Did You Know?

American Bittern populations across much of North America are decreasing in numbers. The decline is attributed to habitat loss and chemical contamination of wetlands. These secretive birds are also sensitive to human disturbance.

Great Blue Heron
Ardea herodias

The long-legged Great Blue Heron has a stealthy, often motionless hunting strategy. It waits for a fish or frog to approach, spears the prey with its bill, then flips its catch into the air and swallows it whole. Herons usually hunt near water, but they also stalk fields and meadows in search of rodents.
• Great Blue Herons settle in communal treetop nests called rookeries. Nesting herons are sensitive to human disturbance, so observe this bird's behaviour from a distance.

Other ID: blue grey overall; long, dark legs.
Breeding: richer colours; plumes streak from crown and throat. *In flight:* black upperwing tips; neck folds back over shoulders; legs trail behind body; slow, steady wingbeats.
Size: L 1.3–1.4 m; W 1.8 m.
Voice: quiet away from the nest; occasional harsh *frahnk frahnk frahnk* during takeoff.
Status: fairly common to locally abundant migrant and breeder; very rare in winter.
Habitat: forages along edges of rivers, lakes and marshes; also in fields and wet meadows.

Similar Birds

Little Blue Heron

Black-crowned
Night-Heron

black plumes
above eye

straight,
yellow bill

long, curving neck
with black markings
on throat

chestnut
brown thighs

Nesting: colonial; adds to stick platform nest over years; nest width can reach 1.2 m; pale bluish green eggs are 64 x 45 mm; pair incubates 4–7 eggs for approximately 28 days.

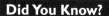

Did You Know?

The Great Blue Heron is the tallest of all herons and egrets in North America.

Look For

In flight, the Great Blue Heron folds its neck back over its shoulders in an S-shape. Similar-looking cranes stretch their necks out when flying.

Turkey Vulture

Cathartes aura

Turkey Vultures are intelligent, playful and social birds. Groups live and sleep together in large trees, or roosts. Some roost sites are over a century old and have been used by the same family of vultures for several generations. • The scientific name *Cathartes aura* means "cleanser" and refers to this bird's affinity for carrion. A vulture's bill and feet are much less powerful than those of eagles, hawks or falcons, which kill live prey. Its red, featherless head may appear grotesque, but this adaptation allows the bird to stay relatively clean while feeding on messy carcasses.

Other ID: *Immature:* grey head. *In flight:* head appears small; silver grey flight feathers; wings are held in a shallow "V"; rocks from side to side when soaring.
Size: L 65–80 cm; W 1.7–1.8 m.
Voice: generally silent; occasionally produces a hiss or grunt if threatened.
Status: uncommon to fairly common migrant and breeder; a few may over-winter.
Habitat: usually flies over open country, shorelines or roads; rarely over forests.

Similar Birds

Black Vulture

Golden Eagle

Bald Eagle (p. 50)

bare, red head

pale, hooked bill

Nesting: in a cave, crevice, log or among boulders; uses no nest material; dull white eggs, irregularly marked with brown or purple, are 71 x 49 mm; pair incubates 2 eggs for up to 41 days.

Did You Know?

A threatened Turkey Vulture will play dead or throw up. The odour of its vomit repulses attackers, much like the odour of a skunk's spray.

Look For

No other bird uses updrafts and thermals in flight as well as the Turkey Vulture. Pilots have reported seeing vultures soaring at 6000 metres.

Osprey

Pandion haliaetus

The large and powerful Osprey is almost always found near water. While hunting for fish, this bird hovers in the air before hurling itself in a dramatic headfirst dive. An instant before striking the water, it rights itself and thrusts its feet forward to grasp its quarry. The Osprey has specialized feet for gripping slippery prey—two toes point forward, two point backward and all are covered with sharp spines. • The Osprey is one of the most widely distributed birds in the world—it is found on every continent except Antarctica.

Other ID: yellow eyes; light crown. *Male:* all-white throat. *Female:* fine, dark "necklace." *In flight:* long wings are held in a shallow "M"; dark "wrist" patches; brown and white tail bands.
Size: *L* 56–64 cm; *W* 1.7–1.8 m.
Voice: series of melodious ascending whistles: *chewk-chewk-chewk;* also a familiar *kip-kip-kip.*
Status: uncommon to fairly common migrant and breeder; a few may over-winter.
Habitat: lakes and slow-flowing rivers and streams; estuaries and bays in migration.

Similar Birds

Bald Eagle (p. 50)

Rough-legged Hawk

dark eye line

grey bill

♀

♂

long wings
extend
past tail

Nesting: on a treetop or artificial structure,
usually near water; massive stick nest is reused
annually; yellowish, brown-blotched eggs are
61 x 46 mm; pair incubates 2–4 eggs for 38 days.

Did You Know?

The Osprey's dark eye
line blocks the glare of
the sun on the water,
enabling it to spot fish
near the water's surface.

Look For

Ospreys build bulky nests on
high, artificial structures such
as communication towers
and utility poles, or on buoys
and channel markers over
water.

Bald Eagle

Sept. '16
"cove Ocean -
front C.G."

Haliaeetus leucocephalus

annapolis Royal

This majestic sea eagle hunts mostly fish and is often found near water. While soaring hundreds of metres high in the air, an eagle can spot fish swimming underwater and small rodents scurrying through the grass. Eagles also scavenge carrion and steal food from other birds.

• Bald Eagles do not mature until their fourth or fifth year—only then will they develop the characteristic white head and tail plumage.

immature

Other ID: *1st year:* dark overall; dark bill; some white in underwings. *2nd year:* dark "bib"; white in underwings. *3rd year:* mostly white plumage; yellow at base of bill; yellow eyes. *4th year:* light head with dark facial streak; variable pale-and-dark plumage; yellow bill; paler eyes.

Size: *L* 76–109 cm; *W* 1.7–2.4 m.

Voice: thin, weak squeal or gull-like cackle: *kleek-kik-kik-kik* or *kah-kah-kah*.

Status: uncommon to locally common year-round resident.

Habitat: seacoasts, estuaries, large lakes and rivers.

Similar Birds

Golden Eagle

Osprey (p. 48)

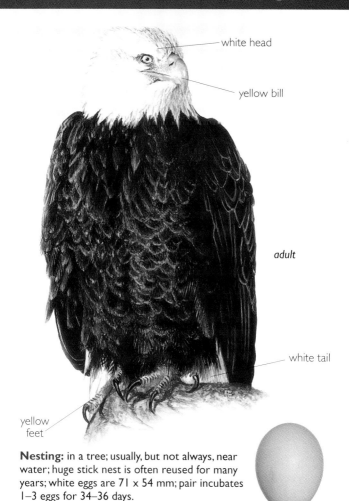

white head

yellow bill

adult

white tail

yellow feet

Nesting: in a tree; usually, but not always, near water; huge stick nest is often reused for many years; white eggs are 71 x 54 mm; pair incubates 1–3 eggs for 34–36 days.

Did You Know?

Bald Eagles add sticks to their nests to renew pair bonds. Nests can be up to 4.5 metres wide, the largest of any North American bird.

Look For

In winter, hundreds of ducks will gather on industrial ponds or other ice-free waters, unknowingly providing an easy meal for hungry Bald Eagles.

Northern Harrier
Circus cyaneus

With its prominent white rump and distinctive slightly upturned wings, the Northern Harrier may be the easiest raptor to identify in flight. Unlike other midsized birds, it often flies close to the ground, relying on sudden surprise attacks to capture prey. • The courtship flight of the Northern Harrier is a spectacle worth watching in spring. The male climbs almost vertically in the air, then stalls and plummets in a reckless dive toward the ground. At the last second he saves himself with a hairpin turn that sends him skyward again.

Other ID: *Male:* blue grey to silver grey upperparts; white underparts; indistinct tail bands, except for 1 dark subterminal band. *Female:* dark brown upperparts; streaky brown-and-buff underparts. *In flight:* long wings and tail; black wing tips; white rump.
Size: *L* 41–61 cm; *W* 1.1–1.2 m.
Voice: generally quiet; high-pitched *ke-ke-ke-ke-ke-ke* near the nest or during courtship.
Status: fairly common migrant; widespread but uncommon breeder; rare winter resident.
Habitat: open country, including fields, wet meadows, cattail marshes, bogs and croplands.

Similar Birds

Rough-legged Hawk

Red-tailed Hawk (p. 56)

Broad-winged Hawk

Red-shouldered Hawk

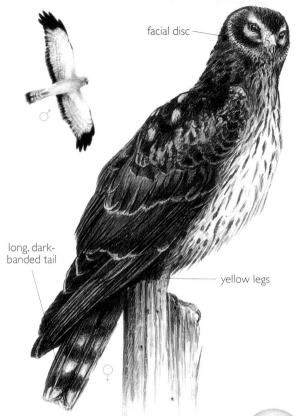

facial disc

♂

long, dark-
banded tail

yellow legs

♀

Nesting: on the ground; usually in tall vegetation or on a raised mound; shallow depression is lined with grass, sticks and cattails; bluish white eggs are 47 x 36 mm; female incubates 4–6 eggs for 30–32 days.

Did You Know?

Britain's Royal Air Force was so impressed by the Northern Harrier's manoeuvrability that it named the Harrier aircraft after this bird.

Look For

The Northern Harrier's owl-like, parabolic facial disc enhances its hearing, allowing this bird to hunt by sound as well as sight.

Sharp-shinned Hawk
Accipiter striatus

After a successful hunt, the small Sharp-shinned Hawk often perches on a favourite "plucking post" with its meal in its razor-sharp talons. This hawk is a member of the *Accipiter* genus, or woodland hawks, and it preys almost exclusively on small birds. Its short, rounded wings, long, rudderlike tail and flap-and-glide flight allow it to manoeuvre through the forest at high speed. • When delivering food to his nestlings, a male Sharp-shinned Hawk takes care not to disturb his mate—she is typically one-third larger than he is and notoriously short-tempered.

Other ID: red eyes. *In flight:* short, rounded wings; dark barring on flight feathers.
Size: *Male:* L 25–30 cm; W 51–61 cm.
Female: L 30–36 cm; W 61–71 cm.
Voice: usually silent; intense, repeated *kik-kik-kik-kik* during the breeding season.
Status: common migrant; fairly common breeder; uncommon winter resident in cities.
Habitat: dense to semi-open forests and large woodlots; occasionally along rivers and in urban areas; favours bogs and dense, moist, coniferous forests for nesting.

Similar Birds

Cooper's Hawk

American Kestrel

Merlin

blue grey crown, back
and upperwings

red horizontal bars
on underparts

long, heavily barred,
square-tipped tail

Nesting: in a conifer tree; builds a new stick nest or uses an abandoned crow nest; brown-blotched, dull white eggs are 38 x 30 mm; female incubates 4–5 eggs for 34–35 days; male feeds the female during incubation.

Did You Know?

As it ages, the Sharp-shinned Hawk's bright yellow eyes become red. This change may signal full maturity to potential mates.

Look For

During winter, Sharp-shinned Hawks may visit backyard bird feeders to prey on feeding sparrows and finches. Watch for their flap-and-glide flight pattern.

Red-tailed Hawk

Buteo jamaicensis

Take an afternoon drive through the country and look for Red-tailed Hawks soaring above the fields. Red-tails are the most common hawks in Atlantic Canada, especially in the southwestern agricultural areas. • In warm weather, these hawks use thermals and updrafts to soar. The pockets of rising air provide substantial lift, which allows migrating hawks to fly for almost 3 kilometres without flapping their wings. On cooler days, resident Red-tails perch on exposed tree limbs, fence posts or utility poles to scan for prey.

Other ID: brown eyes. *In flight:* fan-shaped tail; light underwing flight feathers with faint barring; dark leading edge on underside of wing.

Size: *Male:* L 46–58 cm; W 1.2–1.5 m.
Female: L 51–64 cm; W 1.2–1.5 m.

Voice: powerful, descending scream: *keeearrrr.*

Status: common to abundant year-round resident.

Habitat: open country with some trees; also roadsides or woodlots.

Similar Birds

Rough-legged Hawk

Broad-winged Hawk

Red-shouldered Hawk

Swainson's Hawk

dark upperparts with some white highlights

dark brown band of streaks across belly

red tail

Nesting: in woodlands adjacent to open habitat; bulky stick nest is enlarged each year; brown-blotched, whitish eggs are 59 x 47 mm; pair incubates 2–4 eggs for 28–35 days.

Did You Know?

The Red-tailed Hawk's piercing call is often paired with the image of an eagle in TV commercials and movies.

Look For

Courting pairs will dive at each other, lock talons and tumble toward the earth. They break away only at the last second to avoid crashing into the ground.

Peregrine Falcon
Falco peregrinus

Nothing causes more panic in a flock of ducks or shorebirds than a hunting Peregrine Falcon. This powerful raptor matches every twist and turn the flock makes, then dives to strike a lethal blow.
• Peregrine Falcons represent a successful conservation effort. In the 1960s, the pesticide DDT caused Peregrines to lay eggs with thin shells that broke easily. Peregrine populations declined dramatically until DDT was banned in North America in 1972. Since then, hundreds of captive-bred peregrines have been successfully reintroduced to the wild.

Other ID: blue grey back; yellow feet and cere.
In flight: pointed wings; long, narrow, dark-banded tail.
Size: *Male:* L 38–43 cm; W 94–109 cm.
Female: L 43–48 cm; W 1.1–1.2 m.
Voice: loud, harsh, continuous *cack-cack-cack-cack-cack* near the nest site.
Status: uncommon autumn migrant; rare winter resident and spring migrant; locally rare breeder.
Habitat: lakeshores, river valleys, river mouths, urban areas and open fields.

Similar Birds

Gyrfalcon

Merlin

dark "helmet"

white to buff "chin" and throat

prominent, light underparts with dark, fine spotting and flecking

Nesting: usually on a rocky cliff or cutbank; nest site is often reused and littered with prey remains; white eggs with reddish, brownish or purple blotches are 53 x 41 mm; pair incubates 3–5 eggs for 32–34 days.

Did You Know?

The Peregrine Falcon is the world's fastest bird. In a headfirst dive, it can reach speeds of up to 350 kilometres per hour.

Look For

A pair of peregrines will sometimes nest on the ledge of a tall building, right in the middle of an urban area.

Sora
Porzana carolina

Soras have small bodies and large, chickenlike feet. Even without webbed feet, these unique creatures swim quite well over short distances. • Two rising *or-Ah or-Ah* whistles followed by a strange, descending whinny indicate that a Sora is nearby. Although the Sora is the most common and widespread rail species in North America, it is seldom seen. This secretive bird prefers to remain hidden in dense marshland, but it will occasionally venture into the shallows to search for aquatic insects and molluscs.

Other ID: *Nonbreeding:* less black on face and throat. *Immature:* no black on face; bill is darker; paler underparts.
Size: *L* 20–25 cm; *W* 35 cm.
Voice: clear, 2-note *coo-wee;* alarm call is a sharp *keek;* courtship song begins *or-Ah or-Ah* followed by a maniacal, descending *weee-weee-weee.*
Status: uncommon to common migrant and breeder; a few may overwinter.
Habitat: wetlands with abundant emergent cattails, bulrushes, sedges and grasses.

Similar Birds

Virginia Rail

King Rail

Yellow Rail

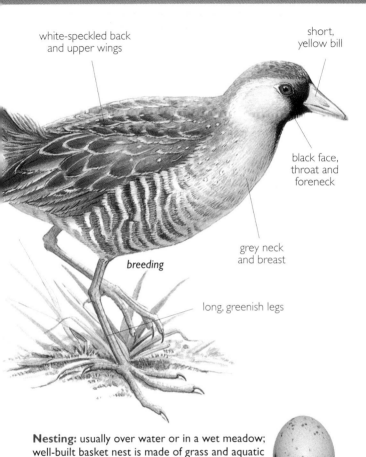

white-speckled back
and upper wings

short,
yellow bill

black face,
throat and
foreneck

grey neck
and breast

breeding

long, greenish legs

Nesting: usually over water or in a wet meadow; well-built basket nest is made of grass and aquatic vegetation; darkly speckled, buff or olive buff eggs are 31 x 22 mm; pair incubates 10–12 eggs for 18–20 days.

Did You Know?

Literally as "thin as a rail," the Sora has a very narrow body that allows it to squeeze through thick stands of cattails.

Look For

The Sora has long legs and very long toes. It bustles through the shallows, darting in and out of the reeds.

Killdeer

Charadrius vociferus

The boisterous Killdeer always attracts attention. It is a gifted actor, well known for its "broken wing" distraction display. When an intruder wanders too close to the nest, it is greeted by an adult Killdeer that cries piteously while dragging a wing and stumbling about as if injured. Most predators take the bait and follow, and once the Killdeer has lured the predator far away from its nest, it miraculously recovers from the injury and flies off with a loud call. Other plovers have similar distraction displays, but the Killdeer's broken wing act is the gold medal winner.

Other ID: brown head; white neck band; brown back and upperwings; white underparts; rufous rump. *Immature:* downy; only 1 breast band.
Size: L 23–28 cm; W 61 cm.
Voice: loud and distinctive *kill-dee kill-dee kill-deer;* variations include *deer-deer.*
Status: common to abundant migrant and breeder; a few may overwinter.
Habitat: open ground, fields, lakeshores, sandy beaches, mudflats, gravel stream-beds, wet meadows and grasslands.

Similar Birds

Semipalmated Plover

Piping Plover

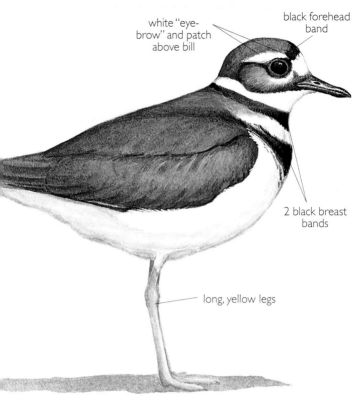

white "eye-brow" and patch above bill

black forehead band

2 black breast bands

long, yellow legs

Nesting: on open ground, in a shallow, usually unlined depression; heavily marked, creamy buff eggs are 36 x 27 mm; pair incubates 4 eggs for 24–28 days; may raise 2 broods.

Did You Know?

In spring, you might hear a European Starling imitate the vocal Killdeer's call.

Look For

The Killdeer has adapted well to urbanization, and it finds golf courses, farms, fields and abandoned industrial areas as much to its liking as shorelines.

Spotted Sandpiper

Actitis macularius

The female Spotted Sandpiper, unlike most other female birds, lays her eggs and leaves the male to tend the clutch. Free of responsibility, she flies off to mate again. Only about one percent of birds display this unusual breeding strategy known as polyandry. Each summer, the female can lay up to four clutches and is capable of producing 20 eggs. As the season progresses, however, available males become harder to find. Come August, there may be seven females for every available male.

Other ID: teeters almost continuously. *Nonbreeding* and *immature:* pure white breast, foreneck and throat; brown bill; dull yellow legs. *In flight:* flies close to the water's surface with very rapid, shallow wingbeats; white upperwing stripe.
Size: *L* 18–20 cm; *W* 38 cm.
Voice: sharp, crisp *eat-wheat, eat-wheat, wheat-wheat-wheat-wheat.*
Status: common migrant and breeder.
Habitat: shorelines, gravel beaches, drainage ditches, swamps and sewage lagoons; occasionally seen in cultivated fields.

Similar Birds

Solitary Sandpiper

Dunlin

Sept. 25/15

campground @
Kouchibouguac Pk.

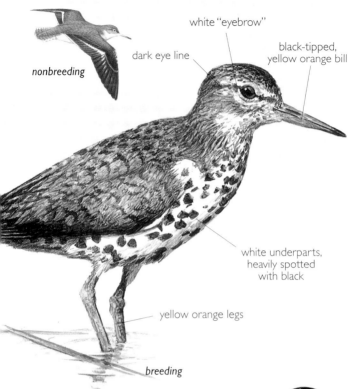

nonbreeding

white "eyebrow"

dark eye line

black-tipped,
yellow orange bill

white underparts,
heavily spotted
with black

yellow orange legs

breeding

Nesting: usually near water; sheltered by vegetation; shallow scrape is lined with grass; darkly blotched, creamy buff eggs are 33 x 24 mm; male incubates the 4 eggs for 20–24 days.

Did You Know?

Sandpipers have four toes: three point forward and one points backward. Plovers, such as the Killdeer, have only three toes.

Look For

Spotted Sandpipers bob their tails constantly on shore and fly with rapid, shallow, stiff-winged strokes.

Sanderling

Calidris alba

This lucky shorebird graces sandy shorelines around the world. The Sanderling skips and plays in the waves, snatching up aquatic invertebrates before they are swept back into the water. On shores where wave action is limited, it resorts to probing mudflats for a meal of molluscs and insects. • To keep warm, Sanderlings seek the company of roosting sandpipers or plovers and turnstones. They will also take a rest from their zigzag dance along a beach to stand with one leg tucked up, a posture that preserves body heat.

Other ID: *Nonbreeding:* pale grey upperparts; black shoulder patch (often concealed). *In flight:* dark leading edge of wing; broad, white stripe across upperwing.

Size: *L* 18–22 cm; *W* 44 cm.

Voice: flight call is a sharp *kip* or *plick*.

Status: common to abundant autumn migrant; fairly common spring migrant; a few may overwinter.

Habitat: sandy and muddy shorelines, cobble and pebble beaches, spits, lakeshores, marshes and reservoirs.

Similar Birds

Baird's Sandpiper

Least Sandpiper

White-rumped Sandpiper

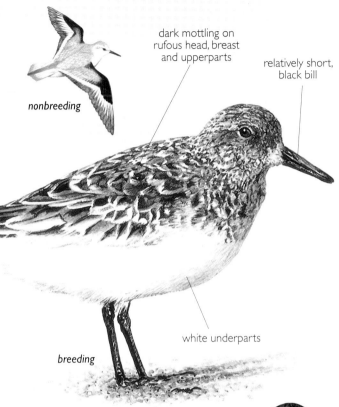

nonbreeding

dark mottling on rufous head, breast and upperparts

relatively short, black bill

white underparts

breeding

Nesting: does not nest in Atlantic Canada; nests on tundra; ground nest among vegetation is lined with leaves and other plant material; olive eggs with variable markings are 36 x 25 mm; mostly the female incubates 4 eggs for 23–24 days.

Did You Know?

The Sanderling breeds across the Arctic and winters on whatever continent it chooses, excluding Antarctica.

Look For

Sanderlings in pale non-breeding plumage reflect a ghostly glow as they forage at night on moonlit beaches.

Wilson's Snipe
Gallinago delicata

A courting Wilson's Snipe makes an eerie, winnowing sound, like a rapidly hooting owl. The male's specialized outer tail feathers vibrate rapidly in the air as he performs daring, headfirst dives high above a wetland. In spring, snipes can be heard displaying day and night. • When flushed from cover, these birds perform a series of aerial zigzags to confuse predators. Because of this habit, hunters who were skilled enough to shoot snipes became known as "snipers," a term later adopted by the military.

Other ID: unmarked, white belly; relatively short legs. *In flight:* quick zigzags on takeoff.
Size: L 27–29 cm; W 46 cm.
Voice: in flight, courtship song is an eerie, accelerating *woo-woo-woo-woo-woo-woo;* often sings *wheat wheat wheat* from an elevated perch; alarm call is a nasal *scaip*.
Status: fairly common to common migrant and breeder; a few may overwinter near water.
Habitat: cattail and bulrush marshes, sedge meadows, poorly drained floodplains, bogs and fens; willow and red-osier dogwood tangles.

Similar Birds

Short-billed Dowitcher

Long-billed Dowitcher

American Woodcock

dark eye stripe

heavily striped head, back and neck

long, sturdy, bicoloured bill

dark barring on breast and flanks

Nesting: usually in dry grass; nest is made of grass, moss and leaves; darkly marked, olive buff to brown eggs are 39 x 28 mm; female incubates 4 eggs for 18–20 days.

Did You Know?

Both parents raise the snipe nestlings, often splitting the brood, with each parent caring for half the chicks.

Look For

A snipe often plunges its entire head underwater while probing the shallows for tasty aquatic critters.

Red-necked Phalarope

Phalaropus lobatus

Flocks of these tiny shorebirds zip about on the open ocean, feeding where there are ocean upwellings. Phalaropes spin and whirl about in tight circles, stirring up tiny aquatic invertebrates. As prey funnels toward the water's surface, these birds daintily pluck them with their needlelike bills. • "Phalarope" is the Greek term for "coot's foot." Like coots and grebes, phalaropes have individually webbed, or lobed, toes, a feature that makes them skilled swimmers.

Other ID: *Breeding female:* blue black head, nape and back; incomplete, white eye ring; white belly; 2 rusty buff stripes on each upperwing. *Breeding male:* less intense colours than female. *Nonbreeding:* black "cap"; broad, dark band from eye to ear; whitish stripes on blue grey upperparts; white underparts.
Size: *L* 18 cm; *W* 38 cm.
Voice: often noisy in migration; soft *krit krit krit*.
Status: common to abundant offshore migrant; rare along coasts and very rare inland.
Habitat: well out to sea, off headlands and around areas of ocean upwellings in the Bay of Fundy.

Similar Birds

Wilson's Phalarope   Red Phalarope

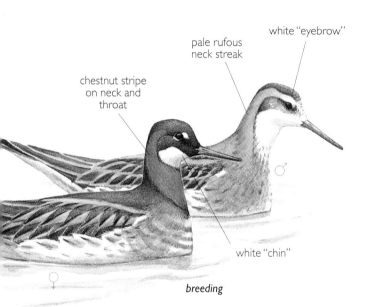

white "eyebrow"

pale rufous
neck streak

chestnut stripe
on neck and
throat

♂

white "chin"

♀

breeding

Nesting: often near water; pair builds a scrape
on a hummock and lines it with grass and lichens;
buff olive, brown-blotched eggs are 30 x 21 mm;
male incubates 4 eggs for 17–21 days.

Did You Know?

Phalaropes are polyan-
drous, meaning that a
female mates with several
males. The female is the
more colourful of the
two sexes.

Look For

Pelagic ferries offer chances
to see Red-necked Phala-
ropes, especially in the waters
off Grand Manan Island and
in Passamaquoddy Bay.

Bonaparte's Gull

Larus philadelphia

This gull's jet-black head in breeding plumage gives it an appealing elegance. With its delicate plumage and behaviour, the small Bonaparte's Gull is nothing like its brash relatives. It avoids landfills, preferring to dine on insects caught in midair or plucked from the water's surface. The Bonaparte's Gull raises its soft, scratchy voice only in excitement, when it spies a school of fish or an intruder. • Whereas other black-headed gulls in Atlantic Canada have orange bills, the Bonaparte's bill is black. The phrase "black-bill Bonaparte's" is a useful memory aid for identification.

Other ID: grey mantle; white underparts.
Nonbreeding: white head; dark ear patch.
In flight: white forewing wedge; black wing tips.
Size: *L* 30–36 cm; *W* 84 cm.
Voice: scratchy, soft *ear ear* while feeding.
Status: common to locally abundant autumn migrant; uncommon spring migrant; very rare winter visitor.
Habitat: offshore upwellings, coastal mudflats, estuaries and salt marshes; occasionally lakeshores.

Similar Birds

Laughing Gull   Black-headed Gull   Franklin's Gull

black head

white eye ring

nonbreeding

black bill

breeding

orange legs

Nesting: not known to nest in Atlantic Canada; shallow nest in a coniferous tree is lined with grass, moss and lichen; pale eggs with variable markings are 49 x 34 mm; pair incubates 2–4 eggs for 24 days.

Did You Know?

This gull was named after Charles-Lucien Bonaparte, a naturalist who made significant ornithological contributions in the 1800s.

Look For

In autumn, flocks of up to several thousand Bonaparte's Gulls gather in places like Head Harbour Passage, New Brunswick, to feast on euphausiid shrimps.

Herring Gull

Larus argentatus

These gulls are as skilled at scrounging handouts
on the beach as their smaller Ring-billed relatives,
but Herring Gulls prefer wilderness areas over
urban settings. It is rare to walk anywhere along
a coastal path without seeing and hearing nesting gulls on the cliff edges
below. • A gull can stand on ice for hours
without freezing its feet. The arteries and veins
in its legs run close together, so that blood
flowing to the extremities warms the cooler blood
travelling back to the core.

Other ID: yellow bill; light grey mantle; white underparts. *Nonbreeding:* white head and nape are washed
with brown. *In flight:* white-spotted, black wing tips.
Size: L 58–66 cm; W 1.2 m.
Voice: loud, buglelike *kleew-kleew;* also
an alarmed *kak-kak-kak.*
Status: abundant migrant; common
to locally abundant breeder; locally
abundant winter visitor.
Habitat: large lakes, wetlands, rivers,
landfills and urban areas.

Similar Birds

Ring-billed Gull   Glaucous Gull   Thayer's Gull   Iceland Gull

KOA in charlottetown Sept. '15

nonbreeding

white head

red spot on lower mandible

breeding

pink legs

Nesting: singly or colonially; on an open beach or island; in a shallow scrape lined with vegetation and sticks; darkly blotched, olive to buff eggs with dark markings are 70 x 48 mm; pair incubates 3 eggs for 31–32 days.

Did You Know?

Although Herring Gulls are skilled hunters, they are opportunistic and scavenge on leftovers in fast-food parking lots and landfills.

Look For

Nestlings use the small red spot on the gull's lower bill as a target. A hungry chick will peck at the spot, cueing the parent to regurgitate its meal.

Great Black-backed Gull

Larus marinus

The Great Black-backed Gull's commanding size and slate grey mantle set it apart from other seabirds, but only adults have this distinctive plumage. For the first four years, immature gulls have dark streaking or mottling, which camouflages them from predators. • Like many marine gulls, Great Black-backed Gulls can drink salt water. Excess salt is removed from their bloodstream by tiny, specialized glands located above their eyes. The salty fluid then dribbles out of their nostrils.

Other ID: *Nonbreeding:* may have faintly streaked nape. *Immature:* variable plumage; mottled grey brown, white and black; black bill or pale, black-tipped bill. *In flight:* grey on trailing edge of underwing; white spots on wing tips.
Size: *L* 76 cm; *W* 1.7 m.
Voice: a harsh *kyow*.
Status: common year-round resident, with populations augmented in winter.
Habitat: harbours, bays, landfills and open water on large lakes and rivers.

Similar Birds

Glaucous Gull

Lesser Black-backed Gull

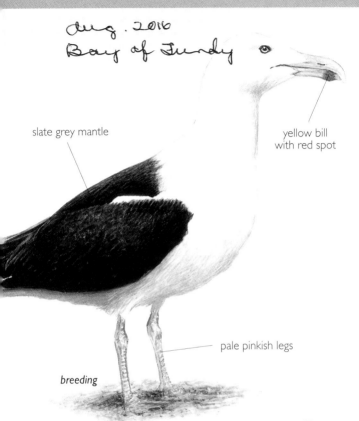

aug. 2016
Bay of Fundy

slate grey mantle

yellow bill
with red spot

pale pinkish legs

breeding

Nesting: usually colonial; on islands, cliff tops or beaches; pair builds a mound of vegetation and debris on the ground; brown-blotched, olive to buff eggs are 78 x 54 mm; pair incubates 2–3 eggs for 27–28 days.

Did You Know?

These opportunistic feeders eat fish, eggs, invertebrates and small mammals. They may also pirate food from other birds or scavenge at landfills.

Look For

A threatened gull will point down its bill, stretch out its neck and walk stiffly to warn away intruders.

Common Tern
Sterna hirundo

Common Terns are sleek, agile birds. They patrol the shorelines of lakes and rivers during spring and autumn, settling in large, noisy nesting colonies in summer. To win a mate, a male will strut through the breeding colony with an offering of fish in his mouth. If a female accepts the suitor's gracious gift, they pair up to nest. Parents defend their nest by diving repeatedly and aggressively at intruders, and will even defecate on offenders to drive them away!

Other ID: white underparts and rump; white tail with grey outer edges. *Nonbreeding:* black nape; lacks black "cap." *In flight:* shallowly forked tail; long, pointed wings; dark grey wedge near lighter grey upperwing tips.
Size: *L* 33–41 cm; *W* 76 cm.
Voice: high-pitched, drawn-out *keee-are;* most commonly heard at colonies.
Status: locally abundant autumn migrant; common spring migrant and breeder.
Habitat: large lakes, open wetlands, slowly moving rivers, islands and beaches.

Similar Birds

Forster's Tern

Arctic Tern

Caspian Tern

black "cap"

black tip on red bill

nonbreeding

red legs

breeding

Nesting: colonial; on an island; in a small scrape lined with pebbles, vegetation or shells; darkly blotched, creamy white eggs are 42 x 30 mm; pair incubates 1–3 eggs for 20–24 days.

Did You Know?

Terns are effortless fliers and impressive long-distance migrants. Once, a Common Tern banded in Great Britain was recovered in Australia.

Look For

Terns hover over the water, then dive headfirst to capture small fish or aquatic invertebrates below the surface.

annapolis Royal
Common Murre
Uria aalge *Sept. '16*

Common Murres spend much of their lives at sea and only come ashore to breed. They nest in huge, tightly packed colonies on isolated coastal cliffs, stacks and offshore islands. Some sites support tens of thousands of birds. • Pelagic boat tours are a fantastic way to see Common Murres in action. Murres can remain beneath the surface for more than a minute and regularly dive to depths of 30 metres. These skilled swimmers use their small wings, webbed feet and sleek, waterproof plumage to pursue fish underwater.

Other ID: *Breeding:* dark brown head and neck. *Nonbreeding:* white neck, "chin" and lower face.
Size: *L* 41–44 cm; *W* 66 cm.
Voice: adults utter a low, harsh *murrr;* dependent juvenile gives a high-pitched, quavering whistle: *FEED-me-now, feed-me-now, feed-me-now!*
Status: common to locally abundant year-round resident; populations may be augmented in winter.
Habitat: *Breeding:* on offshore islands, islets and rocks. *Foraging:* on open ocean from just beyond the surf zone to kilometres offshore.

Similar Birds

| Thick-billed Murre | Razorbill | Dovekie | Black Guillemot (p. 82) |

slender, black bill

deep,
sooty brown
upperparts

white underparts

breeding

Nesting: tightly packed colonies; on bare rock or a flat rocky surface close to water; variably marked and coloured egg is 81 x 50 mm; pair incubates 1 egg for 28–37 days.

Did You Know?

When viewed from above, the murre's dark back blends with the steely sea; from below, its white belly merges with the water's shimmering surface.

Look For

A father will look after his fledgling for about a month. Father-and-chick pairs can sometimes be seen at estuaries in July and August.

Black Guillemot
Cepphus grylle

Unlike other alcids, Black Guillemots prefer to feed in shallow water and may be seen from shore. These birds forage underwater, chasing fish or turning over rocks on the sea floor to expose tasty crustaceans. • Many seabirds become tangled in fishing nets, but oil pollution is a more serious threat. When their feathers become matted with oil, seabirds are less buoyant, unable to fly and lose body heat rapidly. Even a spot of oil the size of a quarter can cause birds to die of hypothermia. • The common name is appropriate only in summer—in winter this bird is mostly white.

Other ID: *Nonbreeding:* white overall, with some black on back, wings and tail. *In flight:* pale underwing.
Size: *L* 33 cm; *W* 53 cm.
Voice: a drawn-out, high-pitched *see-oo* or *swweeeeeer*.
Status: common breeder; uncommon to locally abundant in winter.
Habitat: usually close to shore in relatively shallow water; sometimes far offshore; may feed on freshwater lakes near the coast.

Similar Birds

Common Murre (p. 80)   Thick-billed Murre   Razorbill   Dovekie

nonbreeding

thin, black bill

large, white
wing patch

breeding

reddish legs
and feet

Nesting: singly or in small colonies; along rocky shores, low cliffs and sometimes beaches; nest may be a scrape or a thin layer of pebbles or debris; boldly marked, whitish to pale bluish green eggs are 59 x 40 mm; pair incubates 1–2 eggs for 23–39 days.

Did You Know?

The Black Guillemot and many other cliff-nesting birds have cone-shaped, or pyriform, eggs that will roll in a circle rather than over the rock face.

Look For

Black Guillemots begin breeding as early as April. Nesting colonies are widespread, especially on the Atlantic coasts of Nova Scotia and Newfoundland.

Atlantic Puffin
Fratercula arctica

Famous for its flamboyant bill, the Atlantic Puffin is the main attraction on pelagic birding tours. A puffin can line up more than a dozen small fish crosswise in its bill, possibly using its round tongue and serrated upper mandible to keep the hoard in place. Nonetheless, capturing more fish without losing all previous catches must take great skill!
• Parents abandon their nest burrow when the nestling is about 40 days old. Following a week of fasting, the nestling ventures out to the ocean, fully capable of feeding itself.

Other ID: *Breeding:* black crown, nape and upper-parts; white underparts. *Nonbreeding:* grey bill base lacks yellow border; grey face.
Size: *L* 32 cm; *W* 53 cm.
Voice: usually silent; may give a low, growling *arrr* at breeding sites.
Status: rare to locally abundant breeder; locally common autumn migrant; rare to locally common in winter.
Habitat: *Breeding:* inaccessible coastal cliffs and offshore islands with turf. *In migration* and *winter:* open ocean, occasionally inshore.

Similar Birds

Dovekie

Razorbill

Thick-billed Murre

Common Murre (p. 80)

white face

orange bill with triangular, grey patch, bordered by yellow

breeding

orange legs

Nesting: colonial; in burrows or in crevices among rocks; nest chamber is lined with grass and feathers; dull white egg, possibly marked with brown, is 63 x 45 mm; pair incubates 1 egg for 39–42 days.

Did You Know?

This bird was previously known as "Common Puffin"; other names for it include "Sea Parrot," "Labrador Auk" and "Hatchet-Bill."

Look For

The Atlantic Puffin is the provincial bird of Newfoundland and Labrador. More than half of the North American population breeds at Witless Bay, Newfoundland.

Rock Pigeon
Columba livia

The colourful and familiar Rock Pigeon has an unusual feature: it feeds its young a substance similar to milk. This bird lacks mammary glands, but it produces a nutritious liquid, called "pigeon milk," in its crop. A chick will insert its bill down the adult's throat to reach the thick, protein-rich fluid. • Rock Pigeons are likely the descendants of a Eurasian bird that was first domesticated about 4500 BC. They were introduced to North America in the 17th century by settlers. Most Rock Pigeons now thrive in urban and rural environments, but tall cliffs, which were their original nest sites, provide a more natural habitat for some birds.

Other ID: *In flight:* holds wings in deep "V" while gliding.
Size: *L* 31–33 cm; *W* 71 cm.
Voice: soft, cooing *coorrr-coorrr-coorrr*.
Status: locally abundant year-round resident.
Habitat: urban areas, railway yards, agricultural areas and high cliffs.

Similar Birds

Mourning Dove (p. 88)

Look For

No other "wild" bird varies as much in coloration, a result of semi-domestication and extensive inbreeding over time.

colour is highly variable
(iridescent blue grey, red,
white or tan)

dark-tipped tail

usually has white rump
and orange feet

Nesting: in a barn or on a cliff, bridge or tower; flimsy nest of sticks, grass and other vegetation; glossy white eggs are 39 x 29 mm; pair incubates 2 eggs for 16–19 days; may raise broods year-round.

Did You Know?

Much of our understanding of bird migration, endocrinology, colour genetics and sensory perception comes from experiments involving Rock Pigeons. These birds were also used as message couriers by Caesar and Napoleon.

Mourning Dove
Zenaida macroura

The Mourning Dove's soft cooing, which filters
through broken woodlands and suburban parks,
is often confused with the sound of a hooting owl.
Curious birders who track down the source of the
calls are often surprised to find the streamlined
silhouette of a perched dove. • This popular game
animal is one of the most abundant native birds
in North America. Its numbers and range have
increased because human development creates
more open habitats and food sources, such as
waste grain and bird feeders.

Other ID: buffy, grey brown plumage; small head;
dark bill; sleek body; dull red legs.
Size: *L* 28–33 cm; *W* 46 cm.
Voice: mournful, soft, slow
oh-woe-woe-woe.
Status: common to abundant year-
round in much of Atlantic Canada, and
common migrant elsewhere.
Habitat: open and riparian woodlands,
forest edges, agricultural and suburban
areas and open parks.

Similar Birds

Rock Pigeon (p. 86)

Yellow-billed Cuckoo

Black-billed Cuckoo

dark, shiny patch below ear

black spots on upperwing

pale rosy underparts

long, white-trimmed, tapering tail

Nesting: in a shrub or tree; occasionally on the ground; nest is a fragile, shallow platform of twigs; white eggs are 28 x 22 mm; pair incubates 2 eggs for 14 days.

Did You Know?

The Mourning Dove raises up to six broods each year—more than any other native bird.

Look For

When the Mourning Dove bursts into flight, its wings clap above and below its body. This bird also often creates a whistling sound when flying at high speed.

Great Horned Owl
Bubo virginianus

This highly adaptable and superbly camouflaged hunter has sharp hearing and powerful vision that allow it to hunt at night as well as by day. It will swoop down from a perch onto almost any small creature that moves. • An owl has specially designed feathers on its wings: the leading edge of the first primary feather is serrated rather than smooth. This design interrupts airflow over the wing and allows the owl to fly noiselessly. • Great Horned Owls begin their courtship as early as January, and by February and March, the females are already incubating their eggs.

Other ID: overall plumage varies from light grey to dark brown; heavily mottled grey, brown and black upperparts; yellow eyes; white "chin."
Size: L 46–64 cm; W 91–152 cm.
Voice: breeding call is 4–6 deep hoots: *hoo-hoo-hoooo hoo-hoo* or *Who's awake? Me too;* female gives higher-pitched hoots.
Status: fairly common to common year-round resident.
Habitat: fragmented forests, fields, riparian woodlands, suburban parks and wooded edges of landfills.

Similar Birds

Long-eared Owl

Great Gray Owl

Short-eared Owl

tall, widely spaced "ear" tufts form a triangle with beak

rusty orange facial disc is outlined in black

fine, horizontal barring on breast

Nesting: in another bird's abandoned stick nest, in a tree cavity or on a cliff; adds little or no nest material; dull whitish eggs are 56 x 47 mm; mostly the female incubates 2–3 eggs for 28–35 days.

Did You Know?

The Great Horned Owl has a poor sense of smell, which might explain why it is the only consistent predator of skunks.

Look For

Owls regurgitate pellets that contain the indigestible parts of their prey. You can find these pellets, which are generally clean and dry, under frequently used perches.

Snowy Owl

Bubo scandiacus

Snowy Owls are irregular annual visitors in Atlantic Canada, and their numbers can fluctuate dramatically. When lemming and vole populations crash in the Arctic, large numbers of Snowy Owls venture south to search for food. Feathered to the toes, ghostly white Snowy Owls can remain active even in frigid winter temperatures. Their transparent coat traps heat like a greenhouse. By ruffling their feathers, they also create insulating air pockets to shield them from the cold air. • As Snowy Owls age, their plumage pales—older males are often pure white.

Other ID: *Male:* almost entirely white with very little dark flecking. *Female:* more dark flecking than male. *Immature:* heavier barring than adult female.
Size: *L* 51–69 cm; *W* 1.4–1.7 m (female is noticeably larger).
Voice: quiet during winter.
Status: irregular; rare to locally common winter visitor; a few birds may linger into midsummer at coastal sites.
Habitat: open country, including croplands, meadows, coastal spits and shorelines; often perches on fence posts, buildings and utility poles.

Similar Birds

Great Gray Owl

Northern Hawk Owl

yellow eyes

clean, white face

black bill

dark barring or flecking on breast and upperparts

♀

Nesting: does not nest in Atlantic Canada; breeds on arctic tundra; ground nest is a hollow scrape; white eggs are 57 x 45 mm; female incubates 4–10 eggs for 32–37 days.

Did You Know?

The Snowy Owl may have inspired the first bird painting. Depictions of this owl have been found in prehistoric cave art.

Look For

An owl will often swoop down from its perch and punch through the snow to capture a rodent, leaving an imprint of its outstretched wings.

Common Nighthawk
Chordeiles minor

The Common Nighthawk makes an unforgettable
booming sound as it flies high overhead. In an
energetic courting display, the male dives, then
swerves skyward, making a hollow *vroom* sound
with its wings. • Like other members of the nightjar
family, the Common Nighthawk has adapted to
catch insects in midair: its gaping mouth is surrounded by feather shafts that funnel insects into
its bill. A nighthawk can eat over 2600 insects,
including mosquitoes, blackflies and flying ants,
in one day.

Other ID: *Female:* buff throat. *In flight:* bold, white
"wrist" patches on long, pointed wings; shallowly
forked, barred tail; erratic flight.
Size: L 22–25 cm; W 61 cm.
Voice: frequently repeated, nasal *peent peent;*
wings make a deep, hollow *vroom* during a
courtship dive.
Status: fairly common to locally common autumn migrant; uncommon spring
migrant and breeder.
Habitat: *Breeding:* forest openings, bogs,
rocky outcroppings and gravel rooftops.
In migration: often near water; any area
with large numbers of flying insects.

Similar Birds

Chuck-will's-widow

Whip-poor-will

Brown Creeper

very small bill

white throat
on male

cryptic, mottled
plumage

♂

♂

barred underparts

Nesting: on bare ground; no nest is built; heavily marked, creamy white to buff eggs are 30 x 22 mm; female incubates 2 eggs for about 19 days; both adults feed the young.

Did You Know?

It was once believed that members of the nightjar, or "goatsucker," family could suck milk from the udders of goats, causing the goats to go blind!

Look For

With their short legs and tiny feet, Nighthawks sit lengthwise on tree branches and blend in perfectly with the bark.

Chimney Swift
Chaetura pelagica

Chimney Swifts are the "frequent fliers" of the bird world—they feed, drink, bathe, collect nesting material and even mate while they fly! They spend much of their time catching insects in the skies above Atlantic Canada's urban neighbourhoods. During night migrations, swifts sleep as they fly, relying on changing wind conditions to steer them. • Chimney Swifts have small, weak legs and cannot take flight again if they land on the ground. For this reason, swifts usually cling to vertical surfaces with their strong claws.

Other ID: brown overall; slim body. *In flight:* rapid wingbeats; boomerang-shaped profile; erratic flight pattern.
Size: L 11–14 cm; W 30–33 cm.
Voice: call is a rapid *chitter-chitter-chitter,* given in flight; also gives a rapid series of staccato *chip* notes.
Status: common migrant; fairly common breeder.
Habitat: forages above cities and towns; roosts and nests in chimneys; may nest in tree cavities in more remote areas.

Similar Birds

Northern
Rough-winged Swallow

Bank Swallow

Cliff Swallow

long, thin, pointed, crescent-shaped wings

squared tail

Nesting: often colonial; half-saucer nest of short, dead twigs is attached to a vertical wall; white eggs are 20 x 13 mm; pair incubates 4–5 eggs for 19–21 days.

Did You Know?

Migrating Chimney Swifts can fly at the same altitude as airplanes, approximately 3 kilometres above the ground.

Look For

Swifts frequently nest in brick chimneys or abandoned buildings, and they use saliva to attach their half-saucer nests to the walls.

Ruby-throated Hummingbird

Archilochus colubris

Ruby-throated Hummingbirds bridge the eco-logical gap between birds and bees—they feed on sweet, energy-rich flower nectar and pollinate flowers in the process. A sugarwater feeder or native nectar-producing flowers such as honeysuckle can attract hummingbirds to your backyard. • Each year, Ruby-throated Hummingbirds migrate across the Gulf of Mexico—a nonstop, 800-kilometre journey.

Other ID: irridescent, green back; pale underparts. *Immature:* similar to female.
Size: *L* 9 cm; *W* 11 cm.
Voice: a loud *chick* and other high squeaks; soft buzzing of the wings while in flight.
Status: common migrant, especially in autumn; fairly common breeder.
Habitat: open, mixed woodlands, wetlands, orchards, tree-lined meadows, flower gardens and backyards with trees and feeders.

Similar Birds

Rufous Hummingbird

Look For

Hummingbirds are among the few birds that can fly vertically and in reverse.

thin, needlelike bill

♀

fine, dark
throat streaking
on female

♂

black "chin" with
ruby red throat
on male

dark tail

Nesting: on a horizontal tree limb; tiny, deep cup
nest of plant down and fibres is held together
with spider silk; lichens and leaves are pasted
on the exterior walls; white eggs are 13 x 8 mm;
female incubates 2 eggs for 13–16 days.

Did You Know?

Weighing about as much as a nickel, a hummingbird can
briefly reach speeds of up to 100 kilometres per hour. In
straight-ahead flight, hummingbirds beat their wings up to 80
times per second, and their hearts can beat up to 1200 times
per minute!

Belted Kingfisher
Ceryle alcyon

Perched on a bare branch over a productive pool, the Belted Kingfisher utters a scratchy, rattling call. Then, with little regard for its scruffy hairdo, the "king of the fishers" plunges headfirst into the water and snags a fish or a frog. Back on land, the kingfisher flips its prey into the air and swallows it headfirst. Similar to owls, kingfishers regurgitate the indigestible portion of their food as pellets, which can be found beneath favourite perches. Most of Atlantic Canada's lakes, rivers, streams and marshes are closely monitored by the boisterous Belted Kingfisher.

Other ID: bluish upperparts; small, white patch near eye; straight bill; short legs; white underwings.
Size: L 28–36 cm; W 51 cm.
Voice: fast, repetitive, cackling rattle, like a teacup shaking on a saucer.
Status: common breeder; fairly common migrant; may overwinter along the coast.
Habitat: rivers, large streams, lakes, marshes and beaver ponds, especially near exposed soil banks, gravel pits or bluffs.

Similar Birds

Blue Jay (p. 120)

Look For

The Belted Kingfisher often flies very close to the water, so close, in fact, that its wing-tips may skim the surface.

shaggy crest

white "collar"

♀

rust-coloured "belt"
on female may be
incomplete

♂

blue grey
breast band

Nesting: in a cavity at the end of an earth
burrow; glossy white eggs are 34 x 27 mm;
pair incubates 6–7 eggs for 22–24 days.

Did You Know?

Kingfisher pairs nest on sandy banks, taking turns digging a
tunnel with their sturdy bills and claws. Nest burrows may
measure up to 2 metres long and are often found near
water. Once the young are at least five days old, the parents
return to the nest regularly with small fingerling fish, which
the nestlings eat whole.

Yellow-bellied Sapsucker

Sphyrapicus varius

Yellow-bellied Sapsuckers make their presence known in May, when their irregular tapping echoes throughout our woodlands. Listen for pairs rapping in rhythmic duets. • Sapsuckers drill "wells" in tree trunks, which fill with sweet, sticky sap and attract insects. The sapsuckers eat both the trapped bugs and the pooled sap and must defend the wells from other wildlife, including hummingbirds and small rodents. A pair of sapsuckers might drill many sites within their territory.

Other ID: black-and-white face, back, wings and tail.
Male: red "chin." *Female:* white "chin."
Size: *L* 18–20 cm; *W* 41 cm.
Voice: nasal, catlike *meow;* territorial and courtship hammering has a distinctive 2-speed quality.
Status: fairly common to common migrant and breeder; a few may over-winter.
Habitat: deciduous and mixed forests, especially dry, second-growth woodlands.

Similar Birds

Red-headed
Woodpecker

Downy
Woodpecker (p. 104)

Hairy
Woodpecker

black "bib"

yellow wash on lower breast and belly

red forecrown

large, white wing patch

Nesting: in a cavity lined with wood chips; usually in a live poplar or birch tree with heart rot; white eggs are 22 x 17 mm; pair incubates 5–6 eggs for 12–13 days.

Did You Know?

A sapsucker does not actually suck sap—it laps it up with a tongue that resembles a paintbrush.

Look For

Recently drilled wells that are arranged in parallel horizontal rows indicate that sapsuckers are nearby.

Downy Woodpecker

Picoides pubescens

A pair of Downy Woodpeckers at your backyard bird feeder will brighten a frosty winter day. These approachable little birds are more tolerant of human activities than most other species, and they visit feeders more often than the larger, more aggressive Hairy Woodpeckers. • Like other woodpeckers, the Downy has evolved special features to help cushion the shock of repeated hammering, including strong neck muscles, a flexible, reinforced skull and a brain that is tightly packed in its protective cranium.

Other ID: black eye line and crown; white belly. *Male:* small, red patch on back of head. *Female:* no red patch.
Size: *L* 15–18 cm; *W* 30 cm.
Voice: long, unbroken trill; calls are a sharp *pik* or *ki-ki-ki* or whiny *queek queek*.
Status: common to locally abundant year-round resident.
Habitat: any wooded environment, especially deciduous and mixed forests and areas with tall, deciduous shrubs.

Similar Birds

Hairy
Woodpecker

Yellow-bellied
Sapsucker (p. 102)

American Three-toed
Woodpecker

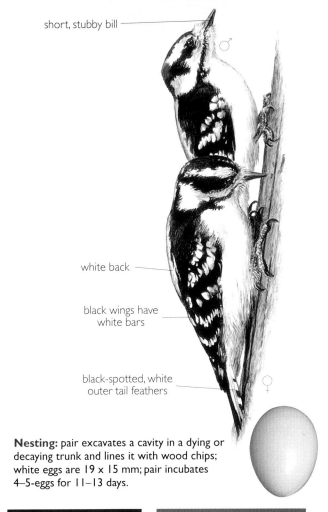

short, stubby bill

♂

white back

black wings have
white bars

black-spotted, white
outer tail feathers

♀

Nesting: pair excavates a cavity in a dying or
decaying trunk and lines it with wood chips;
white eggs are 19 x 15 mm; pair incubates
4–5-eggs for 11–13 days.

Did You Know?

Woodpeckers have feath-
ered nostrils, which filter
out the sawdust produced
by hammering.

Look For

The Downy Woodpecker
uses its small bill to probe
tiny crevices for invertebrates and wood-boring
grubs.

Northern Flicker
Colaptes auratus

Instead of boring holes in trees, the Northern Flicker scours the ground in search of invertebrates, particularly ants. With robinlike hops, it investigates anthills, grassy meadows and forest clearings.
• Flickers often bathe in dusty depressions. The dust particles absorb oils and bacteria that can harm the birds' feathers. To clean themselves even more thoroughly, flickers squash captured ants and preen themselves with the remains. Ants contain formic acid, which kills small parasites on the flickers' skin and feathers.

Other ID: long bill; brownish to buff face; grey crown; white rump. *Male:* black "moustache" stripe. *Female:* no "moustache."
Size: L 32–33 cm; W 51 cm.
Voice: loud, "laughing," rapid *kick-kick-kick-kick-kick-kick; woika-woika-woika* issued during courtship.
Status: abundant migrant and breeder; rare to locally common in winter.
Habitat: *Breeding:* open woodlands and forest edges, fields, meadows, beaver ponds and other wetlands. *In migration* and *winter:* coastal vegetation, offshore islands, urban gardens.

Similar Birds

Red-bellied
Woodpecker

Yellow-bellied
Sapsucker (p. 102)

brown, black-barred back and wings

black "bib"

black-spotted, buff to whitish underparts

red nape crescent

♂

♀

yellow underwings and undertail

Nesting: pair excavates a cavity in a dying or decaying trunk and lines it with wood chips; may also use a nest box; white eggs are 28 x 22 mm; pair incubates 5–8 eggs for 11–16 days.

Did You Know?

The very long tongue of a woodpecker wraps around twin structures in the skull and is stored like a measuring tape in its case.

Look For

Northern Flickers prefer to forage at anthills and may visit their favourite colonies regularly, hammering and probing into the ground to unearth adults and larvae.

Pileated Woodpecker
Dryocopus pileatus

The Pileated Woodpecker, with its flaming red crest, chisel-like bill and commanding size, requires 40 hectares of mature forest as a home territory. In Atlantic Canada, the patchwork of woodlots and small towns limits the availability of continuous habitat, requiring this woodpecker to show itself more often. • A pair will spend up to six weeks excavating a large nest cavity in a dead or decaying tree. Ducks, small falcons, owls and even flying squirrels frequently nest in abandoned Pileated Woodpecker cavities.

Other ID: predominantly black; yellow eyes; white "chin." *Male:* red "moustache." *Female:* no red "moustache"; grey brown forehead.
Size: L 41–48 cm; W 74 cm.
Voice: loud, fast, rolling *woika-woika-woika-woika;* long series of *kuk* notes; loud, resonant drumming.
Status: uncommon to locally common year-round resident.
Habitat: extensive tracts of mature forests; also riparian woodlands or woodlots in suburban and agricultural areas.

Similar Birds

Yellow-bellied
Sapsucker (p. 102)

Red-headed
Woodpecker

Red-bellied
Woodpecker

flaming red crest extends
farther on male

♂ stout, dark bill

white stripe runs
from bill to shoulder

white wing linings

♀

Nesting: pair excavates a cavity in a dying or
decaying trunk and lines it with wood chips;
white eggs are 33 x 25 mm; pair incubates 4 eggs
for 15–18 days.

Did You Know?

A woodpecker's bill
becomes shorter as the
bird ages, so juvenile birds
have slightly longer bills
than adults.

Look For

When foraging, Pileated
Woodpeckers leave large,
rectangular cavities up to
30 centimetres long at the
base of trees.

Olive-sided Flycatcher

Contopus cooperi

The Olive-sided Flycatcher's upright, attentive posture contrasts with its comical song: *quick-three-beers! quick-three-beers!* Like a dutiful parent, this flycatcher changes its tune during nesting, when it more often produces an equally enthusiastic *pip-pip-pip.* • Olive-sided Flycatchers nest high in the forest canopy. Far above the forest floor, they have easy access to an abundance of flying insects, including honeybees, adult wood-boring beetles and bark beetles.

Other ID: dark upper mandible; dull yellow orange base to lower mandible; inconspicuous eye ring; white tufts on sides of rump.
Size: *L* 18–20 cm; *W* 33 cm.
Voice: *Male:* song is a chipper and lively *quick-three-beers!*, with the second note highest in pitch; descending *pip-pip-pip* when excited.
Status: uncommon to locally fairly common breeder; rare to fairly common migrant.
Habitat: semi-open mixed and coniferous forests near water; prefers burnt areas and wetlands.

Similar Birds

Eastern Wood-Pewee

Eastern Phoebe

Eastern Kingbird (p. 112)

olive grey to
olive brown
upperparts

light throat
and belly

dark olive
grey "vest"

Nesting: high in a conifer, usually on a branch far from the trunk; nest of twigs and plant fibres is bound with spider silk; darkly spotted, white to pinkish buff eggs are 22 x 16 mm; female incubates 3 eggs for 14–17 days.

Did You Know?

Olive-sided Flycatchers are fierce nest defenders and will harass and chase off squirrels and other predators.

Look For

A big-headed silhouette on the tip of a mature conifer or dead branch may well belong to this feisty flycatcher.

Eastern Kingbird
Tyrannus tyrannus

The Eastern Kingbird fearlessly attacks crows, hawks and even humans that pass through its territory, pursuing and pecking at them until it feels the threat has passed. No one familiar with the Eastern Kingbird's pugnacious behaviour will refute its scientific name, *Tyrannus tyrannus*. • These kingbirds are common and widespread. On a drive in the country you will likely spot at least one Eastern Kingbird sitting on a fence or utility wire. These birds can also be very common close to the coast in migration, especially in late April and early May.

white-tipped tail

Other ID: black bill; no eye ring; white underparts; black legs.
Size: *L* 22 cm; *W* 38 cm.
Voice: call is a quick, loud, chattering *kit-kit-kitter-kitter;* also a buzzy *dzee-dzee-dzee.*
Status: common to very common migrant and breeder.
Habitat: rural fields with scattered trees or hedgerows, clearings in fragmented forests, open roadsides, burnt areas and near human settlements.

Similar Birds

Olive-sided Flycatcher
(p. 110)

Eastern Wood-Pewee

Least Flycatcher

thin, orange red crown
(rarely seen)

small head crest

dark grey to black
upperparts

Nesting: on a horizontal limb, stump or upturned tree root; cup nest is made of weeds, twigs and grass; darkly blotched, white to pinkish white eggs are 24 x 18 mm; female incubates 3–4 eggs for 14–18 days.

Did You Know?

This bird reveals its gentler side in a quivering, butterfly-like courtship flight.

Look For

Eastern Kingbirds rarely walk or hop on the ground—they prefer to fly, even for very short distances.

Northern Shrike
Lanius excubitor

One of the most vicious predators in the bird world, the Northern Shrike relies on its sharp, hooked bill to catch and kill small birds or rodents, which it spots from treetop perches. This bird possesses extremely acute vision: one shrike spotted flying bumblebees at least 90 metres away! The Northern Shrike's tendency to impale its prey on thorns and barbs for later consumption has earned it the name "Butcher Bird." The scientific name means "watchful butcher," which appropriately describes the shrike's foraging behaviour. • Each autumn, Northern Shrikes retreat from their taiga breeding grounds and visit Atlantic Canada.

Other ID: black tail and wings; pale grey upperparts.
In flight: white wing patches.
Size: L 25 cm; W 37 cm.
Voice: usually silent; occasionally gives a long grating "laugh": *raa-raa-raa-raa*.
Status: uncommon and erratic migrant and winter visitor.
Habitat: open country, including fields, shrubby areas, forest clearings and roadsides.

Similar Birds

Loggerhead Shrike

Northern Mockingbird

Northern Wheatear

black "mask" does not extend above hooked bill

juvenile

finely barred, pale underparts

white outer tail feathers

Nesting: nests on the coast of Labrador; in a spruce, willow or shrub; bulky nest is made of sticks, bark and moss; variably marked, greenish white to pale grey eggs are 29 x 19 mm; female incubates 4–7 eggs for 15–17 days.

Did You Know?

Shrikes are the world's only true carnivorous songbirds. Africa and Eurasia boast the greatest diversity of shrike species.

Look For

Winter feeding stations tempt many shrikes to test their hunting skills on the feeding birds.

Red-eyed Vireo
Vireo olivaceus

The male Red-eyed Vireo can out-sing any of his courting neighbours. Capable of delivering about 40 phrases per minute, one tenacious male set a record by singing 21,000 phrases in one day! Though you may still hear the Red-eyed Vireo singing five or six hours after other songbirds have ceased for the day, this bird is not easy to spot concealed in its olive brown plumage among the foliage of deciduous trees. Its unique red eyes, unusual among songbirds, are even trickier to notice without a good pair of binoculars.

Other ID: black-bordered, olive "cheek"; olive green upperparts; white to pale grey underparts.
Size: *L* 15 cm; *W* 24 cm.
Voice: call is a short, scolding *neeah*.
Male: song is a series of quick, continuous, variable phrases with pauses in between: *look-up, way-up, tree-top, see-me, here-l-am!*
Status: common to very common migrant and breeder.
Habitat: deciduous woodlands with a shrubby understorey.

Similar Birds

Philadelphia Vireo

Blue-headed Vireo

Tennessee Warbler

blue grey crown

white "eyebrow"

dark eye line

red eyes

breeding

Nesting: in a tree or shrub; hanging cup nest is made of grass, roots, spider silk and cocoons; darkly spotted, white eggs are 20 x 14 mm; female incubates 4 eggs for 11–14 days.

Did You Know?

Often parasitized by Brown-headed Cowbirds, these vireos respond by abandoning their nests or raising the cowbird young with their own.

Look For

The Red-eyed Vireo perches with a hunched stance and hops with its body turned diagonally to the direction of travel.

Gray Jay
Perisoreus canadensis

The friendly, mischievous Gray Jay sports a dark grey cloak and a long, elegant tail. This bold bird forms a strong pair bond, and after an absence, partners will seek each other out and touch or nibble bills. Gray Jays lay their eggs and begin incubation as early as late February, allowing the young to get a head start on learning to find and store food. These birds cache food for winter, and their specialized salivary glands coat the food with a sticky mucus that helps to preserve the meal and renders it unappetizing to other birds and forest mammals.

Other ID: dark bill; fluffy, pale grey breast and belly; white undertail coverts.
Size: *L* 28–33 cm; *W* 45 cm.
Voice: calls include a soft, whistled *quee-oo*, a chuckled *cla-cla-cla* and a *churr*; also imitates other birds.
Status: uncommon to common year-round resident.
Habitat: dense and open coniferous and mixed forests, bogs and fens; picnic sites and campgrounds.

Similar Birds

Northern Shrike (p. 114)   Loggerhead Shrike   Northern Mockingbird

white forehead, "cheek" and throat

dark grey nape and upperparts

fairly long tail

Nesting: in a conifer; insulated nest is made of plant fibres, roots, moss, twigs, feathers and fur; speckled, pale grey to greenish eggs are 29 x 21 mm; female incubates 3–4 eggs for 17–22 days.

Did You Know?

The nickname "Whiskey Jack" is derived from this jay's Algonquin name, *wis-kat-jon;* other names include "Canada Jay" and "Camp Robber."

Look For

Gray Jays are easiest to find in campgrounds and picnic areas, where they will win your admiration as they steal your lunch! They also visit suburban feeders in winter.

Blue Jay
Cyanocitta cristata

In Atlantic Canada, the Blue Jay is the only member of the corvid family dressed in blue. It is easily recognizable with its white-flecked wing feathers and sharply defined facial features. This jay can be quite aggressive when competing for sunflower seeds and peanuts at backyard feeding stations and rarely hesitates to drive away smaller birds, squirrels or even cats when it feels threatened. Even the Great Horned Owl is not too formidable a predator for a group of these brave, boisterous mobsters to harass.

Other ID: blue upperparts; white underparts; black bill.
Size: L 28–31 cm; W 40 cm.
Voice: noisy, screaming *jay-jay-jay;* nasal *queedle queedle queedle-queedle* sounds like a muted trumpet; often imitates various sounds, including calls of other birds.
Status: common to abundant migrant and winter resident; common breeder.
Habitat: mixed and deciduous forests, agricultural areas, scrubby fields and townsites.

Similar Birds

Belted Kingfisher (p. 100)

Eastern Bluebird

blue crest

black "necklace"

white bars
and flecking
on wings

dark bars and
white corners
on blue tail

Nesting: in a tree or tall shrub; pair builds a
bulky stick nest; greenish, buff or pale grey eggs,
spotted with olive and brown, are 28 x 20 mm;
pair incubates 4–5 eggs for 16–18 days.

Did You Know?

Blue Jays store food col-
lected from feeders in
trees and other places
for later use.

Look For

What may appear to be
a dozen or so individual
regulars at a feeder are often
actually three or four loose
flocks "doing the rounds."

American Crow
Corvus brachyrhynchos

The noise that most often emanates from this treetop squawker seems unrepresentative of its intelligence. However, this wary, clever bird is also an impressive mimic, able to whine like a dog and laugh or cry like a human. • These abundant birds are ecological generalists: they eat a diversity of foods and adapt to a variety of habitats. They are common throughout Atlantic Canada in summer but generally congregate in the more southern parts of our region in winter, when they often form large flocks called "murders."

Other ID: glossy, purple black plumage; black bill and legs.
Size: *L* 43–53 cm; *W* 94 cm.
Voice: distinctive, far-carrying, repetitive *caw-caw-caw*.
Status: common to locally abundant year-round resident, with noticeable local migration in winter.
Habitat: urban areas, agricultural fields and other open areas with scattered woodlands; also marshes, lakes and rivers in densely forested areas.

Similar Birds

Common Raven (p. 124)

Black-billed Magpie

slim, sleek head
and throat

square-shaped
tail

Nesting: in a tree or on a utility pole; large
stick-and-branch nest is lined with fur and soft
plant materials; darkly blotched, grey green to
blue green eggs are 41 x 29 mm; female incubates
4–6 eggs for about 18 days.

Did You Know?

Crows are family-oriented,
and the young from the
previous year may help
their parents raise the
current year's nestlings.

Look For

To distinguish this bird from
the Common Raven, look for
the squared tail and slimmer
bill of the American Crow.

Common Raven
Corvus corax

The Common Raven is the largest of all passerines, or perching birds. It soars with a wingspan comparable to that of hawk's, travelling along coastlines, over deserts, along mountain ridges and even on arctic tundra. The range of this adaptable bird encompasses much of the Northern Hemisphere, so if you travel to some parts of Europe, Asia or North Africa, you may be greeted by the familiar sight of the Common Raven. • Ravens are glorified in native cultures, perhaps because they exhibit behaviours that were once thought of as exclusively human.

Other ID: all-black plumage; heavy, black bill; rounded wings.
Size: *L* 61 cm; *W* 1.3 m.
Voice: deep, guttural, far-carrying, repetitive *craww-craww* or *quork quork* among other vocalizations.
Status: common year-round resident; locally abundant in winter.
Habitat: coniferous and mixed forests and woodlands; townsites, campgrounds and landfills.

Similar Birds

American Crow (p. 122)

Look For

When working as a pair to confiscate a meal, one raven may act as the decoy while the other steals the food.

shaggy throat

wedge-shaped tail

Nesting: on a ledge, bluff or utility pole or in a tall coniferous tree; large stick-and-branch nest is lined with fur and soft plant materials; variably marked, greenish eggs are 50 x 33 mm; female incubates 4–6 eggs for 18–21 days.

Did You Know?

Breeding ravens maintain loyal, lifelong pair bonds, which are reinforced each winter in courtship chases consisting of drag races, barrel rolls, dives and tumbles. Pairs endure everything from food scarcity to harsh weather and cooperate to raise the young. Ravens can live up to 40 years and sometimes even longer.

Horned Lark
Eremophila alpestris

An impressive, high-speed, plummeting courtship dive would blow anybody's hair back, or in the case of the Horned Lark, its two unique black "horns." Long before the snow is gone, this bird's tinkling song will be one of the first you hear introducing spring. • Horned Larks are often abundant at road-sides, searching for seeds, but an approaching vehicle usually sends them flying into an adjacent field. When these birds visit in winter, you can spot them in farmers' fields or spy them at the beach visiting with Snow Buntings and Lapland Longspurs.

Other ID: *Male:* light yellow to white face; pale throat; dull brown upperparts. *Female:* duller plumage.
Size: *L* 18 cm; *W* 30 cm.
Voice: call is a tinkling *tsee-titi* or *zoot;* flight song is a long series of tinkling, twittered whistles.
Status: common to locally abundant migrant and winter resident; locally uncommon breeder, mostly along the coast.
Habitat: *Breeding:* open areas, including pastures, croplands, airfields and coastal barrens. *In migration* and *winter:* also shorelines and roadside ditches.

Similar Birds

Snow Bunting

Lapland Longspur

American Pipit

small black "horns" (rarely raised)

black line under eye extends from bill to "cheek"

black breast band

dark tail with white outer tail feathers

Nesting: on the ground; in a shallow scrape lined with grass, plant fibres and roots; brown-blotched, grey to greenish white eggs are 23 x 16 mm; female incubates 3–4 eggs for 10–12 days.

Did You Know?

One way to distinguish a sparrow from a Horned Lark is by the method of travel: Horned Larks walk, whereas sparrows hop.

Look For

The Horned Lark's dark tail contrasts with its light brown body and belly and is a great field mark.

Tree Swallow
Tachycineta bicolor

Tree Swallows, our most common summer swallows, are often seen perched beside their fence-post nest boxes. When conditions are favourable, these busy birds are known to return to their young 10 to 20 times per hour (about 140 to 300 times a day!). This nearly ceaseless activity provides observers with plenty of opportunities to watch and photograph these birds in action. • In the evening and during light rains, small groups of foraging Tree Swallows sail gracefully above rivers and wetlands, catching stoneflies, mayflies and caddisflies.

Other ID: white underparts; no white on "cheek." *Female:* slightly duller. *Immature:* brown above; white below. *In flight:* long, pointed wings.
Size: *L* 14 cm; *W* 37 cm.
Voice: alarm call is a metallic, buzzy *klweet. Male:* song is a liquid, chattering twitter.
Status: common migrant and breeder.
Habitat: open areas, such as beaver ponds, marshes, lakeshores, field fence-lines, townsites and open woodlands.

Similar Birds

| Purple Martin | Eastern Kingbird (p. 112) | Bank Swallow | Barn Swallow (p. 130) |

small bill

iridescent, dark blue
or green head and
upperparts

shallowly
forked tail

Nesting: in a tree cavity or nest box lined
with weeds, grass and feathers; white eggs are
19 x 13 mm; female incubates 4–6 eggs for up to
19 days.

Did You Know?

When Tree Swallows leave
the nest to forage, they
frequently cover their
eggs with feathers from
the nest.

Look For

In the bright sunshine, the
back of the Tree Swallow
appears blue; prior to autumn
migration the back appears
green.

Barn Swallow
Hirundo rustica

When you encounter this bird, you might first notice its distinctive, deeply forked tail—or you might just find yourself repeatedly ducking to avoid the dives of a protective parent. Barn Swallows once nested on cliffs, but their cup-shaped mud nests are now found more frequently on human-made structures, such as barns, boathouses and areas under bridges. The messy young and aggressive parents often motivate people to remove nests just as the nesting season is beginning, but this bird's close association with humans allows us to observe the normally secretive reproductive cycle of birds.

Other ID: blue black upperparts; long, pointed wings.
Size: *L* 18 cm; *W* 38 cm.
Voice: continuous, twittering chatter: *zip-zip-zip* or *kvick-kvick*.
Status: common to abundant migrant and breeder.
Habitat: open rural and urban areas where bridges, culverts and buildings are found near water.

Similar Birds

Cliff Swallow

Purple Martin

Tree Swallow (p. 128)

rufous throat
and forehead

black "necklace"

rust- to buff-coloured
underparts

long, deeply
forked tail

Nesting: singly or in small, loose colonies; on a human-made structure under an overhang; half or full cup nest is made of mud, grass and straw; brown-spotted, white eggs are 20 x 14 mm; pair incubates 4–7 eggs for 13–17 days.

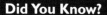

Did You Know?

The Barn Swallow is a natural pest controller, feeding on insects that are often harmful to crops and livestock.

Look For

Barn Swallows roll mud into small balls and build their nests one mouthful of mud at a time.

Black-capped Chickadee

Poecile atricapillus

You can catch a glimpse of this incredibly sociable chickadee at any time of the year in Atlantic Canada. In winter, Black-caps join the company of kinglets, nuthatches, creepers and small woodpeckers to feed; in spring and autumn, they join mixed flocks of vireos and warblers. While observing their antics at feeders, you may even be able to entice a Black-capped Chickadee to the palm of your hand with the help of a sunflower seed. • During cold nights, chickadees enter into a hypothermic state, lowering their body temperature and heartbeat considerably to conserve energy.

Other ID: white underparts; light buff sides and flanks; dark legs.
Size: *L* 13–15 cm; *W* 20 cm.
Voice: call is a chipper, whistled *chick-a-dee-dee-dee*; song is a slow, whistled *swee-tee* or *fee-bee*.
Status: common year-round resident.
Habitat: deciduous and mixed forests, riparian woodlands, wooded urban parks; backyard feeders.

Similar Birds

Boreal Chickadee

Blackpoll Warbler

black "cap" and "bib"

white "cheek"

grey back and wings

white edging on wing feathers

Nesting: pair excavates a cavity in a rotting tree or stump; occasionally uses a birdhouse; cavity is lined with fur, feathers, moss, grass and cocoons; finely speckled, white eggs are 15 x 12 mm; female incubates 6–8 eggs for 12–13 days.

Did You Know?

Black-capped Chickadees are thought to possess amazing memories. They can relocate seed caches up to a month after they are hidden!

Look For

The Black-capped Chickadee sometimes feeds while hanging upside-down, giving it the chance to grab a treat another bird may not be able to reach.

Red-breasted Nuthatch

Sitta canadensis

The Red-breasted Nuthatch may look a little like a woodpecker, but its view of the world could be considered somewhat dizzying. This interesting bird, with its distinctive black eye line and red breast, moves down tree trunks headfirst, cleaning up the seeds, insects and nuts that woodpeckers may have overlooked. • The odd name "nuthatch" comes from this bird's habit of wedging large nuts into crevices, then using its bill to hammer the nuts open.

Other ID: white "cheek"; straight bill; short tail.
Male: black crown. *Female:* dark grey crown.
Size: *L* 11 cm; *W* 21 cm.
Voice: call is a slow, repeated, nasal *yank yank yank;* also a short *tsip.*
Status: fairly common year-round resident; occasionally locally abundant in migration.
Habitat: *Breeding:* spruce-fir and pine forests. *In migration* and *winter:* mixed woodlands, especially near bird feeders.

Similar Birds

White-breasted
Nuthatch

Black-capped
Chickadee (p. 132)

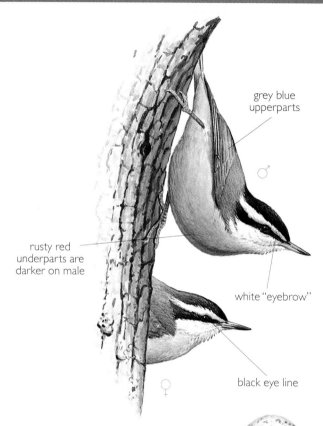

grey blue
upperparts

♂

rusty red
underparts are
darker on male

white "eyebrow"

♀

black eye line

Nesting: excavates a cavity or uses an abandoned woodpecker nest; nest is made of bark shreds, grass and fur; brown-spotted white eggs are 15 × 12 mm; female incubates 5–6 eggs for about 12 days.

Did You Know?

These birds smear their nest-cavity entrances with sap to keep away ants and other insects that can transmit fungal infections or parasitize nestlings.

Look For

The Red-breasted Nuthatch visits feeders, but you may catch only a glimpse of its red belly as it grabs a seed and darts away to eat it in private.

Brown Creeper
Certhia americana

The cryptic Brown Creeper is never easy to find, often going unnoticed until a flake of bark suddenly takes the shape of a bird. A frightened creeper will freeze and flatten itself against a tree trunk, becoming nearly invisible. • The Brown Creeper uses its long, stiff tail feathers to prop itself up while spiraling up vertical tree trunks, searching for hidden invertebrates. When it reaches the upper branches, it floats down to the base of a neighbouring tree to begin another foraging ascent.

Other ID: brown upperparts with buffy white streaks; white underparts; rufous rump.
Size: *L* 13 cm; *W* 19 cm.
Voice: song is a faint, high-pitched *trees-trees-trees see the trees;* call is a high *tseee.*
Status: fairly common year-round resident.
Habitat: mature forests and woodlands, especially in wet areas with large, dead trees.

Similar Birds

Common Nighthawk
(p. 94)

Northern
Flicker (p. 106)

White-throated
Sparrow

downcurved bill

white "eyebrow"

long, pointed
tail feathers

Nesting: under loose bark; nest of grass and
conifer needles is woven together with spider
silk; brown-spotted, whitish eggs are 15 x 12 mm;
female incubates 5–6 eggs for 14–17 days.

Did You Know?

There are many species
of creepers in Europe
and Asia, but the Brown
Creeper is the only mem-
ber of its family found in
North America.

Look For

The Brown Creeper occa-
sionally visits urban parks
and suet feeders in winter.

Winter Wren
Troglodytes troglodytes

The upraised, mottled brown tail of the Winter
Wren matches the gnarled, upturned roots and
decomposing tree trunks it calls home. Although
it blends well with its habitat, you may wonder
how something so small could have such vocal
magnitude—it boldly lays claim to its territory
with its call and distinctive, melodious song.
• Although the male Winter Wren contributes to
raising the family, defending the nest and finding
food for the nestlings, he sleeps elsewhere at night,
in an unfinished nest.

Other ID: dark brown upperparts; lighter brown
underparts.
Size: *L* 10 cm; *W* 14 cm.
Voice: *Male:* song is a warbled, tinkling series of
quick trills and twitters, up to 10 seconds long;
call is a sharp *chip-chip*.
Status: common migrant and breeder;
rare winter visitor.
Habitat: moist boreal forest, spruce
bogs, cedar swamps and mixed forests
dominated by mature pine and hemlock;
often near water; also tuckamore and
shrubbery near the coast in migration
and winter.

Similar Birds

House Wren   Marsh Wren   Sedge Wren   Carolina Wren

very short, stubby, upraised tail

fine, pale "eyebrow"

prominent, dark barring on flanks

Nesting: in a natural cavity, under bark or under upturned tree roots; nest is made of twigs, moss, grass and fur; male builds up to 4 "dummy" nests; white eggs with reddish brown dots are 18 x 13 mm; female incubates 5–7 eggs for 14–16 days.

Did You Know?

The Winter Wren, often called the "Jenny Wren," can sustain its song for 10 seconds using up to 113 tones.

Look For

This bird has a habit of bobbing its entire body up and down as if it were doing push-ups.

Golden-crowned Kinglet

Regulus satrapa

The dainty Golden-crowned Kinglet is not much bigger than a hummingbird, and when it gleans for insects, berries and sap in the forest canopy, it is prone to unique hazards such as perishing on the burrs of burdock plants. • "Pishing" and squeaking sounds might lure these songbirds into an observable range. Their behavioural traits, such as their perpetual motion and chronic wing flicking, can help identify Golden-crowns from a distance.

Other ID: black border around crown; black eye line; dark "cheek"; olive back; darker wings and tail; light underparts.
Size: *L* 10 cm; *W* 19 cm.
Voice: song is a faint, high-pitched, accelerating *tsee-tsee-tsee-tsee, why do you shilly-shally?*; call is a very high-pitched *tsee tsee tsee*.
Status: common to abundant year-round resident.
Habitat: *Breeding:* mature coniferous forests. *In migration* and *winter:* coniferous, deciduous and mixed forests; sometimes visits urban parks and gardens.

Similar Birds

Ruby-crowned Kinglet

Black-capped Chickadee (p. 132)

Boreal Chickadee

reddish orange crown

♂

yellow crown

2 white wing bars

white "eyebrow"

♀

Nesting: usually in a spruce or other conifer; hanging nest is made of moss, lichen, twigs and leaves; pale buff eggs, spotted with grey and brown, are 13 x 10 mm; female incubates 8–9 eggs for 14–15 days.

Did You Know?

Derived from the Latin word for "king," *Regulus* is a fitting scientific name for a bird that wears a golden crown!

Look For

Golden-crowns are often joined by flocks of chickadees, Red-breasted Nuthatches and Brown Creepers at the tops of spruces, pines and firs.

Swainson's Thrush
Catharus ustulatus

This bird, once known as the "Olive-backed Thrush," is usually the last singer heard at nightfall. The Swainson's Thrush shares the speckled breast of other Atlantic Canada thrushes, as well as the habit of foraging on the ground for insects and other invertebrates. But unlike its next-of-kin, it may hover-glean from the airy heights of trees like a warbler or vireo. • The Swainson's Thrush is a wary bird and often gives its sharp warning call from a distance, offering little chance to be seen.

Other ID: brown grey upperparts; white belly and undertail coverts.
Size: *L* 18 cm; *W* 31 cm.
Voice: song is a slow, rolling, rising spiral: *Oh, Aurelia will-ya, will-ya will-yeee;* call is a sharp *wick* or *prit.*
Status: common to very common migrant; common breeder.
Habitat: edges and openings of coniferous and mixed boreal forests to treeline; prefers moist areas with spruce and fir.

Similar Birds

Gray-cheeked Thrush

Bicknell's Thrush

Hermit Thrush

Veery

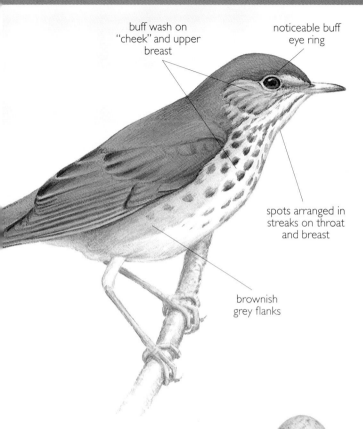

buff wash on "cheek" and upper breast

noticeable buff eye ring

spots arranged in streaks on throat and breast

brownish grey flanks

Nesting: usually in a shrub or small tree; cup nest is made of grass, moss and leaves, lined with with fur and soft fibres; brown-spotted pale blue eggs are 22 × 17 mm; female incubates 3–4 eggs for 12–14 days.

Did You Know?

The Swainson's song has rapid, flutelike notes that spiral upward, rather than downward like the songs of other *Catharus* thrushes.

Look For

In the breeding season, you can frequently spot this bird's silhouette perched against a colourful sunset sky at the top of the tallest tree in its territory.

American Robin
Turdus migratorius

Come March, the familiar song of the American Robin may wake you early if you are a light sleeper. This abundant bird adapts easily to urban areas and often works from dawn until after dusk when there is a nest to be built or hungry, young mouths to feed. The American Robin's bright red belly contrasts with its dark head and wings to make this bird easy to identify, even for a nonbirder. • Fermenting fruit on trees may convince these birds to stay for winter in the south of our region, where they gather in roosts to drink the intoxicating juices.

Other ID: incomplete, white eye ring; grey brown back; white under-tail coverts.
Size: *L* 25 cm; *W* 43 cm.
Voice: song is an evenly spaced warble: *cheerily cheer-up cheerio;* call is a rapid *tut-tut-tut.*
Status: abundant year-round resident.
Habitat: residential lawns and gardens, pastures, urban parks, broken forests, bogs and river shorelines.

Similar Birds

Varied Thrush

Look For

A hunting robin with its head tilted to the side isn't listening for prey—it is actually looking for movements in the soil.

black head

black-tipped,
yellow bill

dark grey head

brick red breast is
darker on male

white throat
is streaked
with black

♂

♀

Nesting: in a tree or shrub; cup nest is built
of grass, moss, bark and mud; light blue eggs
are 28 x 20 mm; female incubates 4 eggs for
11–16 days; raises up to 3 broods per year.

Did You Know?

American Robins do not use nestboxes, but prefer platforms
for their nests. The female stays busy raising up to three
broods per year, and her young are easily distinguishable with
their dishevelled plumage and heavily spotted underparts.

Gray Catbird

Dumetella carolinensis

This accomplished mimic may fool you if you hear it shuffling through underbrush and dense riparian shrubs, calling its catlike *meow*. Its mimicking talents are further enhanced by its ability to sing two notes at once, using each side of its syrinx individually. • In a competitive nesting habitat of sparrows, robins and cowbirds, the Gray Catbird vigilantly defends its territory. It will destroy the eggs and nestlings of other songbirds and take on an intense defensive posture if approached, screaming and even attempting to hit an intruder.

Other ID: dark grey overall; black eyes, bill and legs.
Size: L 11–14 cm; W 28 cm.
Voice: calls include a catlike *meoww* and a harsh *check-check;* song is a variety of warbles, squeaks and mimicked phrases interspersed with a *mew* call.
Status: uncommon to fairly common migrant and breeder; very rare winter visitor.
Habitat: dense thickets, brambles, shrubby or brushy areas and hedgerows, often near water.

Similar Birds

Gray Jay (p. 118)

Northern Mockingbird

Townsend's Solitaire

black "cap"

long tail is dark
grey to black

chestnut undertail
coverts

Nesting: in a dense shrub or thicket; bulky cup nest is made of twigs, leaves and grass; greenish blue eggs are 23 x 17 mm; female incubates 4 eggs for 12–15 days.

Did You Know?

The watchful female Gray Catbird can recognize a Brown-headed Cowbird egg and will remove it from her nest.

Look For

If you catch a glimpse of this bird during the breeding season, watch the male raise his long slender tail into the air to show off his rust-coloured undertail coverts.

European Starling
Sturnus vulgaris

The European Starling did not hesitate to make itself known across North America after being released in New York's Central Park in 1890 and 1891. These highly adaptable birds not only took over the nest sites of native cavity nesters, such as Tree Swallows and Red-headed Woodpeckers, but they learned to mimic the sounds of Killdeers, Red-tailed Hawks, Soras and meadowlarks. European Starlings are now very common birds in Atlantic Canada. Look for them in massive evening roosts under bridges or on buildings. • European Starlings have a varied diet that includes agricultural pests, berries and grains.

Other ID: dark eyes; short, squared tail.
Nonbreeding: feather tips are heavily spotted with white and buff.
Size: *L* 22 cm; *W* 40 cm.
Voice: variety of whistles, squeaks and gurgles; imitates other birds.
Status: abundant year-round resident.
Habitat: agricultural areas, townsites, woodland edges, landfills and roadsides.

Similar Birds

Rusty Blackbird

Brewer's Blackbird

Brown-headed
Cowbird (p. 174)

iridescent, purple black
head, neck and breast

yellow bill

glossy, green back
with buffy spots

greenish black
underparts

breeding

Nesting: in an abandoned woodpecker cavity, natural cavity or nest box; nest is made of grass, twigs and straw; bluish to greenish white eggs are 30 x 21 mm; female incubates 4–6 eggs for 12–14 days.

Did You Know?

This bird was brought to New York as part of the local Shakespeare society's plan to introduce birds mentioned in their favourite author's writings.

Look For

The European Starling looks somewhat like a blackbird. Look for the starling's comparably shorter tail and bright yellow bill to help you identify it.

Cedar Waxwing
Bombycilla cedrorum

With its black "mask" and slick "hairdo," the Cedar Waxwing has a heroic look. The splendid personality of this bird is reflected in its amusing antics after it gorges on fermented berries and in its gentle courtship dance. To court a mate, the gentlemanly male hops toward a female and offers her a berry. The female accepts the berry and hops away, then stops, and hops back toward the male to offer him the berry in return. • Planting native berry-producing trees and shrubs in your backyard can attract Cedar Waxwings, and may even encourage them to nest in your area.

Other ID: brown upperparts; yellow wash on belly; grey rump; white undertail coverts.
Size: *L* 18 cm; *W* 30 cm.
Voice: faint, high-pitched, trilled whistle: *tseee-tseee-tseee.*
Status: common migrant and breeder; irregularly common in winter.
Habitat: wooded residential parks and gardens, overgrown fields, forest edges, second-growth, riparian and open woodlands.

Similar Birds

Bohemian Waxwing

Look For

The yellow tail band and "waxy" red wing tips get their colour from pigments in the berries that these birds eat.

cinnamon crest

black "mask"

small red "drops" on wings

yellow terminal tail band

Nesting: in a tree or shrub; cup nest is made of twigs, moss and lichen; darkly spotted, bluish to greyish eggs are 22 x 16 mm; female incubates 3–5 eggs for 12–16 days.

Did You Know?

Flocks of handsome Cedar Waxwings take turns gorging on berries from bushes or trees in late summer and autumn. If a bird's crop is full, it will continue to pluck fruit and pass it down the line of birds as if it were in a bucket brigade, until the fruit is gulped down by a still-hungry bird.

Yellow Warbler
Dendroica petechia

The widely distributed Yellow Warbler arrives in May singing its *sweet-sweet* song and flitting from branch to branch in search of juicy caterpillars, aphids and beetles. This bright yellow bird is often mistakenly called a "Wild Canary." • The Yellow Warbler is frequently parasitized by the Brown-headed Cowbird and can recognize cowbird eggs. Rather than tossing out the foreign eggs, it will build another nest overtop the old eggs or abandon the nest completely. Occasionally, cowbirds strike repeatedly—a stack of five warbler nests was once found!

Other ID: bright yellow body; yellowish legs; black bill and eyes. *Female:* may have faint, red breast streaks.
Size: *L* 13 cm; *W* 20 cm.
Voice: song is a fast, frequently repeated *sweet-sweet-sweet summer sweet.*
Status: common migrant and breeder.
Habitat: moist, open woodlands with dense, low scrub; shrubby areas and riparian woodlands; usually near water.

Similar Birds

Orange-crowned Warbler   American Goldfinch   Wilson's Warbler   Common Yellowthroat

bright yellow highlights on
dark yellow olive tail and wings

red breast streaks

♀

♂

breeding

Nesting: in a deciduous tree or shrub; female
builds a cup nest of grass, weeds and shredded
bark; darkly speckled, greyish or greenish white
eggs are 17 x 13 mm; female incubates eggs for
11–12 days.

Did You Know?

The Yellow Warbler has
an amazing geographical
range. It is found throughout North America and
on islands in Central and
South America.

Look For

Yellow Warblers usually
arrive in early May with the
first main wave of spring
warblers.

American Redstart
Setophaga ruticilla

Known as "Butterfly Bird" in some parts of its range, the American Redstart rarely, if ever, sits still. Its Latin American name, *candelita*, meaning "little torch," also describes it perfectly. Not only are the male's bright orange patches the colour of a glowing flame, but the bird never ceases to flicker, even when perched. • In its seemingly nonstop pursuit of prey, the American Redstart flushes insects with the flash of colour from its wings or tail. Then it uses its broad bill and rictal bristles, the short whiskerlike feathers around its mouth, to capture insects like an expert flycatcher.

Other ID: *Male:* white belly and undertail coverts. *Female:* white underparts.
Size: *L* 13 cm; *W* 19 cm.
Voice: male's song is a highly variable series of *tseet* or *zee* notes at different pitches; call is a sharp, sweet *chip*.
Status: common migrant and breeder.
Habitat: shrubby woodland edges; open and semi-open forests with a regenerating deciduous understorey; often near water.

Similar Birds

Baltimore Oriole

Orchard Oriole

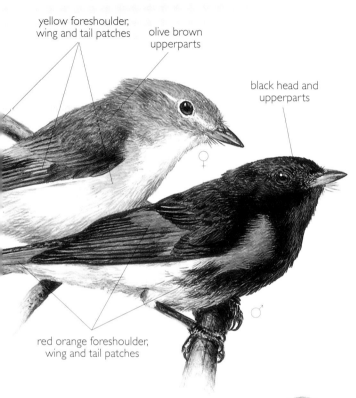

yellow foreshoulder, wing and tail patches

olive brown upperparts

black head and upperparts

♀

♂

red orange foreshoulder, wing and tail patches

Nesting: in a shrub or sapling; female builds open cup nest of plant down, bark shreds, grass and rootlets; brown-marked, whitish eggs are 16 x 12 mm; female incubates 4 eggs for 11–12 days.

Did You Know?

This bird's high-pitched, lisping, trilly songs are so variable that identifying an American Redstart by song alone is a challenge to birders of all levels.

Look For

Even when an American Redstart is perched, its colour-splashed tail sways rhythmically back and forth.

Ovenbird
Seiurus aurocapilla

Even the sharpest human eye will have trouble spotting the Ovenbird's immaculately concealed nest along hiking trails and bike paths. An incubating female is usually confident enough in the camouflage of her ground nest that she will choose to sit tight rather than flee in the presence of danger. Furthermore, some females have as many as three mates to call on for protection and to help feed the young. Despite these evolutionary adaptations, forest fragmentation and Brown-headed Cowbird parasitism have reduced this bird's nesting success.

Other ID: olive brown upperparts; no wing bars; white undertail coverts; pink legs.
Size: *L* 15 cm; *W* 24 cm.
Voice: loud, distinctive *tea-cher tea-cher Tea-CHER Tea-CHER,* increasing in speed and volume; night song is bubbly, warbled notes, often ending in *teacher-teacher;* call is a brisk *chip, cheep* or *chock.*
Status: common migrant; fairly common to common breeder.
Habitat: *Breeding:* undisturbed, mature forests with a closed canopy and little understorey; often in ravines and riparian areas. *In migration:* dense riparian shrubbery and thickets; coastal woodlands.

Similar Birds

Northern Waterthrush

Louisiana Waterthrush

Swainson's Thrush
(p. 142)

rufous crown
bordered by black

white eye ring

heavy, dark streaking on white
breast, sides and flanks

Nesting: on the ground; female builds a domed, oven-shaped nest of grass, twigs, bark and dead leaves lined with animal hair; white eggs with grey and brown spots are 20 x 15 mm; female incubates 4–5 eggs for 11–13 days.

Did You Know?

The name "Ovenbird" refers to this bird's unusual nest, which is shaped like a Dutch oven.

Look For

In summer, this bird remains hidden in tangles of low shrubs or among conifer branches. However, the male's loud *tea-cher* song will give away his presence.

Scarlet Tanager
Piranga olivacea

The vibrant red of a breeding male Scarlet Tanager may catch your eye in Atlantic Canada's wooded ravines and migrant stopover sites. Because this tanager is more likely to reside in forest canopies, birders tend to hear the Scarlet Tanager before they see it. Its song, a sort of slurred version of the American Robin's, is a much-anticipated sound that announces the arrival of this colourful long-distance migrant. The Scarlet Tanager has the northernmost breeding grounds and longest migration route of all tanager species, and it is the only tanager that routinely nests in Atlantic Canada.

Other ID: *Female:* uniformly olive upperparts; yellow underparts; greyish brown wings; yellow eye ring.
Size: *L* 18 cm; *W* 29 cm.
Voice: song is a series of 4–5 sweet, clear, whistled phrases; call is *chip-burrr* or *chip-churrr*.
Status: uncommon migrant; rare to locally uncommon breeder; a few overwinter.
Habitat: fairly mature, upland deciduous and mixed forests; also coastal shrubbery in migration.

Similar Birds

Summer Tanager   Northern Cardinal

pure black
wings and tail

pale bill

bright red body

♀   ♂

Nesting: high in a deciduous tree; female builds a flimsy, shallow cup nest of grass, weeds and twigs; brown-spotted, pale blue green eggs are 23 × 16 mm; female incubates 2–5 eggs for 12–14 days.

Did You Know?

In Central and South America, there are over 200 tanager species in every colour imaginable.

Look For

Scarlet Tanagers forage in the forest understorey in cold, rainy weather, making them easier to observe.

Chipping Sparrow
Spizella passerina

Though you may spot the relatively tame Chipping Sparrow singing from a high perch, it commonly nests at eye level, so you can easily watch its breeding and nest-building rituals. You can take part in the building of this bird's nest by leaving samples of your pet's hair, or your own, around your backyard.
• This bird's song is very similar to that of the Dark-eyed Junco. Listen for a slightly faster, drier and less musical series of notes to identify the Chipping Sparrow.

Other ID: *Breeding:* mottled brown upperparts; light grey, unstreaked underparts; dark bill. *Nonbreeding:* paler crown with dark streaks; brown "eyebrow" and "cheek"; pale lower mandible.
Size: L 13–15 cm; W 21 cm.
Voice: song is a rapid, dry trill of *chip* notes; call is a high-pitched *chip*.
Status: common to abundant migrant and breeder; a few overwinter.
Habitat: open conifers or mixed wood-land edges; yards and gardens with tree and shrub borders.

Similar Birds

American Tree Sparrow

Swamp Sparrow

Field Sparrow

prominent rufous "cap"

white "eyebrow"

black eye line

pale wing bars

breeding

Nesting: usually at midlevel in a coniferous tree; female builds a cup nest of grass and rootlets lined with hair; pale blue, sparsely marked eggs are 18 x 13 mm; female incubates 4 eggs for 11–12 days.

Did You Know?

The Chipping Sparrow is the most common and widely distributed migrating sparrow in North America.

Look For

This sparrow visits feeders and forages on lawns for the seeds of grass, dandelions and clovers.

Song Sparrow
Melospiza melodia

Although its plumage is unremarkable, the well-named Song Sparrow is among the great songsters of the bird world. By the time a young male Song Sparrow is a few months old, he has created a courtship tune of his own, having learned the basics of melody and rhythm for his song from his father and male rivals. • Mild winters in Atlantic Canada can convince these songsters to stick around. The presence of a well-stocked backyard feeder may be a fair trade for a sweet song in the dead of winter.

Other ID: white jaw line with dark "moustache" stripes; mottled brown upperparts; rounded tail tip.
Size: *L* 14–18 cm; *W* 20 cm.
Voice: song is 1–4 introductory notes, such as *sweet sweet sweet,* followed by buzzy *towee,* then a short, descending trill; call is a short *tsip* or *tchep.*
Status: common to abundant migrant and breeder; uncommon winter visitor.
Habitat: willow shrub lands, riparian thickets, forest openings and pastures, all often near water.

Similar Birds

Fox Sparrow   Lincoln's Sparrow   Savannah Sparrow

greyish face

dark crown with pale central stripe

brown line behind eye

heavy brown streaks converge at central breast spot

Nesting: usually on the ground or in a low shrub; female builds an open cup nest of grass, weeds and bark strips; brown-blotched, bluish or greenish white eggs are 22 x 17 mm; female incubates 3–5 eggs for 12–14 days.

Did You Know?

Although female songbirds are not usually vocal, the female Song Sparrow will occasionally sing a tune of her own.

Look For

The Song Sparrow pumps its long, rounded tail in flight. It also often issues a high-pitched *seet* flight call.

Sept./15 Sugarloaf Park

Dark-eyed Junco
Junco hyemalis

You might feel some sympathy for this sparrow, picking at the scraps under your backyard feeder, but the Dark-eyed Junco prefers to forage on the ground, avoiding the crowd of noshing chickadees, nuthatches and jays. The conical shape of the junco's bill enables it to use maximum force to crack seeds.
• Most juncos migrate south for winter, but even during the coldest years in Atlantic Canada, you might find a few lingering "Snow Birds" here.

Other ID: *Female:* is grey brown where the male is slate grey.
Size: L 14–17 cm; W 23 cm.
Voice: song is a long, dry trill; call is a smacking *chip* note, often given in series.
Status: common to abundant migrant and winter visitor; common breeder.
Habitat: *Breeding:* coniferous and mixed forests; shrubby, regenerating areas. *In migration* and *winter:* shrubby woodland borders, backyard feeders.

Similar Birds

Eastern Towhee

Look For

The Dark-eyed Junco will flash its distinctive white outer tail feathers as it rushes for cover after being flushed.

pale pink bill

dark slate grey
overall

white outer
tail feathers

white belly
and undertail
coverts

♂

"Slate-coloured Junco"

Nesting: on the ground, usually concealed;
female builds a cup nest of twigs, grass, bark
shreds and moss; brown-marked, whitish to
bluish eggs are 19 x 14 mm; female incubates
3–5 eggs for 12–13 days.

Did You Know?

In 1973, the American Ornithologists' Union grouped five
junco species, all of which interbreed where their ranges
meet, into a single species called the Dark-eyed Junco. The
subspecies present in Atlantic Canada is the plain-looking
"Slate-coloured Junco."

Rose-breasted Grosbeak
Pheucticus ludovicianus

The Rose-breasted Grosbeak's stout, conical bill gives its head a more rounded appearance and "gros," which is French for "large," certainly describes this bird's distinctive bill. Mating grosbeaks appear pleasantly affectionate toward each other, often touching bills during courtship and after absences. Both parents incubate the eggs and occasionally sing their boisterous, whistled tune from the nest, introducing the young to a world of melody. When conditions permit, Rose-breasted Grosbeaks may produce two broods in a summer.

Other ID: pale, conical bill. *Male:* white underparts and rump; white corners on dark tail. *Female:* thin, pale crown stripe; brown upperparts; buff underparts with dark brown streaking; dark tail.
Size: *L* 18–21 cm; *W* 32 cm.
Voice: song is a long, melodious series of whistled notes; call is a distinctive squeak.
Status: uncommon to fairly common migrant and breeder; a few overwinter.
Habitat: deciduous and mixed forests; sometimes visits feeders in early winter.

Similar Birds

Purple Finch

Savannah Sparrow

Lapland Longspur

bold, whitish "eyebrow"

dark wings with small white patches

black "hood" and back

red breast and inner underwings

♀

♂

breeding

Nesting: fairly low in a tree or tall shrub, often near water; mostly the female builds a cup nest lined with rootlets and hair; pale greenish blue eggs spotted with reddish brown are 25 x 18 mm; pair incubates 3–5 eggs for 13–14 days.

Did You Know?

Though the female lacks the formal dress of the male, she joins him in song, an unusual trait for most female songbirds.

Look For

The Rose-breasted Grosbeak generally forages high in the forest canopy in summer, but it is drawn to a birder's eye level in autumn by an abundance of ripened berries.

Indigo Bunting
Passerina cyanea

The vivid electric blue male Indigo Bunting is one of the most spectacular birds in Atlantic Canada. The bunting arrives in April or May and favours raspberry thickets as nest sites. Dense, thorny stems keep most predators at a distance and the berries are a good food source. • The male is a persistent singer, vocalizing even through the heat of a summer day. A young male doesn't learn his couplet song from his parents, but from neighbouring males during his first year on his own.

Other ID: beady black eyes; black legs; no wing bars. *Male:* bright blue overall; black lores. *Female:* soft brown overall; whitish throat.
Size: *L* 14 cm; *W* 20 cm.
Voice: song consists of paired warbled whistles: *fire-fire, where-where, here-here, see-it see-it;* call is a quick *spit*.
Status: irregularly common migrant; rare and very local breeder; a few overwinter.
Habitat: deciduous forest and woodland edges, regenerating forest clearings, orchards and shrubby fields.

Similar Birds

Blue Grosbeak

Eastern Bluebird

darker blue
on head

grey,
conical bill

wings and tail may
show some black

faint brown streaks
on breast

♂

♀

breeding

Nesting: in a small tree, shrub or within a vine tangle; female builds a cup nest of grass, leaves and bark strips; unmarked, white to bluish white eggs are 19 x 14 mm; female incubates 3–4 eggs for 12–13 days.

Did You Know?

Females choose the most melodious males as mates, because these males can usually establish territories with the finest habitat.

Look For

The Indigo Bunting will land midway on a stem of grass or a weed and shuffle slowly toward the seed head, bending down the stem to reach the seeds.

Red-winged Blackbird
Agelaius phoeniceus

The male Red-winged Blackbird wears his bright red shoulders like armour—together with his short, raspy song, they are key in defending his territory from rivals. In field experiments, males with black painted over their red shoulders soon lost their territories. • These birds are early spring arrivals, often returning to Atlantic Canada in mid-March. It isn't hard to spot the polygynous males perched atop cattails in roadside ditches and wetlands, but the cryptically coloured females usually remain inconspicuous on their nests.

Other ID: *Male:* black overall. *Female:* mottled brown upperparts; pale "eyebrow."
Size: *L* 18–24 cm; *W* 33 cm.
Voice: song is a loud, raspy *konk-a-ree* or *ogle-reeeee*; calls include a harsh *check* and high *tseert*; female gives a loud *che-che-che chee chee chee.*
Status: abundant migrant; common breeder; rare to locally uncommon winter visitor.
Habitat: *Breeding:* cattail marshes, wet meadows and ditches, croplands and shoreline shrubs. *In migration* and *winter:* farmlands; urban ponds, shrubbery and feeders.

Similar Birds

Brewer's
Blackbird

Rusty
Blackbird

Brown-headed
Cowbird (p. 174)

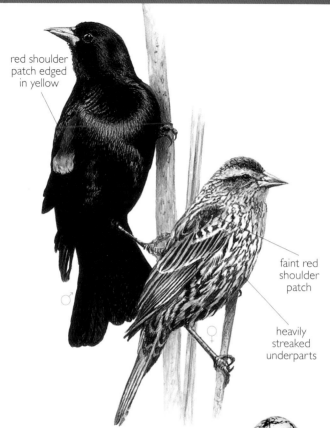

red shoulder
patch edged
in yellow

faint red
shoulder
patch

heavily
streaked
underparts

♂

♀

Nesting: colonial; in cattails or shoreline bushes; female builds an open cup nest of dried cattail leaves lined with fine grass; darkly marked, pale blue green to grey eggs are 25 x 18 mm; female incubates 3–4 eggs for 10–12 days.

Did You Know?

Some scientists believe that the Red-winged Blackbird is the most abundant bird in North America.

Look For

Red-winged Blackbirds gather in immense flocks in agricultural areas and open fields in winter.

Eastern Meadowlark
Sturnella magna

The drab dress of most female songbirds lends them and their nestlings protection during the breeding season, but the female Eastern Meadowlark uses a different strategy. Her "V" necklace and bright yellow throat and belly create a colourful distraction to lead predators away from the nest. A female flushed from the nest while incubating her eggs will often abandon the nest, and though she will never abandon her chicks, her extra vigilance following a threat usually results in less frequent feeding of nestlings.

Other ID: yellow underparts; mottled brown
_upperparts; long, sharp bill; blackish crown stripes and eye line border pale "eyebrow" and median crown stripe; dark streaking on white sides.
Size: *L* 23–24 cm; *W* 35 cm.
Voice: song is a rich series of 2–8 melodic, clear, slurred whistles: *see-you at school-today* or *this is the year;* gives a rattling flight call and a high, buzzy *dzeart.*
Status: rare to uncommon migrant and breeder; rare winter visitor.
Habitat: grassy meadows and pastures, some croplands, weedy fields, grassy roadsides and old orchards; also coastal barrens in migration and winter.

Similar Birds

Western Meadowlark

Dickcissel

yellow lores

white jaw line

short, wide tail with white outer tail feathers

broad, black breast band

breeding

Nesting: in a concealed depression on the ground; female builds a domed grass nest, woven into surrounding vegetation; heavily spotted, white eggs are 28 x 20 mm; female incubates 3–7 eggs for 13–15 days.

Did You Know?

The name suggests that this bird is a lark, but it is actually a brightly coloured member of the blackbird family. Its silhouette reveals its blackbird features.

Look For

The Eastern Meadowlark often whistles its proud song from fence posts and power lines. Song is the best way to tell it apart from the very rare Western Meadowlark.

Brown-headed Cowbird
Molothrus ater

These nomads historically followed bison herds across the prairies (they now follow cattle), so they didn't stay in one area long enough to build and tend a nest. Instead, cowbirds lay their eggs in other birds' nests, relying on unsuspecting mothers to incubate the eggs and feed the aggressive young. Orioles, warblers, vireos and tanagers are among the most affected. Increased livestock farming and fragmentation of forests has encouraged the expansion of the cowbird's range, and it now parasitizes more than 140 bird species.

Other ID: dark eyes; thick, conical bill; short, squared tail.
Size: *L* 15–20 cm; *W* 30 cm.
Voice: song is a high, liquidy gurgle: *glug-ahl-whee* or *bubbloozeee;* call is a squeaky, high-pitched *seep, psee or-wee-tse-tse* or fast, chipping *ch-ch-ch-ch-ch-ch.*
Status: uncommon to locally abundant winter visitor; uncommon to locally common migrant and breeder.
Habitat: agricultural and residential areas, landfills, campgrounds and areas near cattle.

Similar Birds

Rusty Blackbird   Brewer's Blackbird   Common Grackle

pale throat

dark brown head

light brown
underparts with
faint streaking

♀

iridescent, green
blue body plumage
looks glossy black

♂

Nesting: does not build a nest; female lays
up to 40 eggs a year in the nests of other birds,
usually 1 egg per nest; brown-speckled, whitish
eggs are 21 x 16 mm; eggs hatch after 10–13
days.

Did You Know?

Cowbirds don't form pair
bonds, but a male will perform a courtship display:
he points his bill skyward,
fans his tail and wings and
utters a loud *squeek*.

Look For

When cowbirds feed in
flocks, they hold their back
ends up high, with their tails
sticking straight up in the air.

White-winged Crossbill

Loxia leucoptera

The unique bill of the White-winged Crossbill is shared by only one other bird in North America: the Red Crossbill. The crossed mandibles are adapted to pry open cones to eat the seeds of spruce, fir and tamarack—in fact, they are so well adapted for extracting seeds from cones that a single bird can eat up to 3000 conifer seeds a day! When White-winged Crossbills overwinter, they gather in flocks at the tops of spruce trees, creating showers of conifer cone skeletons and a crackling chatter of bills.

Other ID: *Male:* black wings and tail. *Female:* faint, brownish streaking on body; dark wings and tail.
Size: *L* 15–17 cm; *W* 27 cm.
Voice: song is a high-pitched series of warbles, trills and chips; call is a series of harsh, questioning *cheat* notes, often given in flight.
Status: uncommon to fairly common, transient year-round resident.
Habitat: coniferous forests; occasionally townsites and deciduous forests.

Similar Birds

Red Crossbill

Pine Grosbeak

Purple Finch

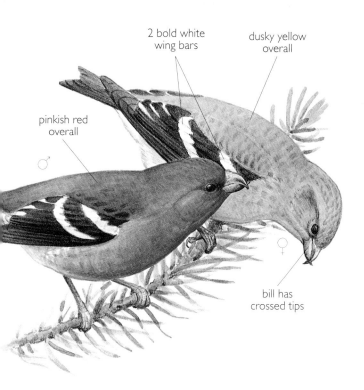

2 bold white
wing bars

dusky yellow
overall

pinkish red
overall

♂

bill has
crossed tips

♀

Nesting: on an outer branch in a conifer; female builds an open cup nest of twigs, grass, bark shreds, leaves and moss, lined with rootlets and hair; pale blue green eggs spotted with brown and lavender are 21 x 15 mm; female incubates 2–4 eggs for 12–14 days.

Did You Know?

White-winged Crossbills can breed in any season, as long as food supplies are abundant enough to support the energetic demands of nesting.

Look For

You might catch a glimpse of White-winged Crossbills licking the salt from winter roads, a dangerous habit that occasionally results in death.

Common Redpoll
Carduelis flammea

These tiny northern birds sometimes make a modest appearance, showing up in winter in small groups of a dozen or fewer. Other winters, they flock in the hundreds, gleaning waste grain from bare fields or stocking up at winter feeders. • A large surface area relative to a small internal volume puts the Common Redpoll at risk of freezing in low temperatures, but a high intake of food and the insulating layer of warm air trapped by its fluffed feathers keeps this songbird from dying of hypothermia.

Other ID: yellowish bill; streaked upperparts; notched tail.
Size: *L* 13 cm; *W* 22 cm.
Voice: song is a twittering series of trills; calls are a soft *chit-chit-chit-chit* and a faint *swe-eet*.
Status: fairly common but local year-round breeding resident; uncommon to locally abundant erratic, irruptive migrant and winter visitor.
Habitat: *Breeding:* coastal and alpine tundra; locally in alder thickets.
Winter: coastal barrens and scrubby growth, open fields, roadsides and forest edges.

Similar Birds

Hoary Redpoll

House Finch

red forecrown

black "chin"

pinkish red breast
on male

lightly streaked
sides, flanks and
undertail coverts

♀

♂

nonbreeding

Nesting: low in a shrub or dwarf spruce; occasionally in a grass clump; open cup nest is made of fine twigs, grass and moss; darkly speckled, pale blue eggs are 17 x 13 mm; female incubates 4–5 eggs for 12 days.

Did You Know?

The Common Redpoll has diverticula, or pockets, in its esophagus, in which it can store seeds for later digestion.

Look For

Common Redpolls spend a lot of time at feeders in winter and prefer birch and alder seeds because of their high calorie content.

American Goldfinch
Carduelis tristis

Like tiny rays of sunshine, American Goldfinches cheerily flutter over weedy fields, gardens and along roadsides. It is hard to miss their jubilant *po-ta-to-chip* call and their distinctive, undulating flight style. • Because these acrobatic birds regularly feed while hanging upside-down, finch feeders have been designed with the seed opening below the perches. These feeders discourage more aggressive House Sparrows, which feed upright, from stealing the seeds. Use niger or millet seeds to attract American Goldfinches to your bird feeder.

Other ID: *Nonbreeding male:* olive brown back; yellow-tinged head; grey underparts.
Size: *L* 11–14 cm; *W* 23 cm.
Voice: song is a long, varied series of trills, twitters, warbles and hissing notes; calls include *po-ta-to-chip* or *per-chic-or-ee* (often delivered in flight) and a whistled *dear-me, see-me*.
Status: fairly common to common year-round resident; local in eastern Newfoundland.
Habitat: weedy fields, woodland edges, meadows, riparian areas, parks and gardens.

Similar Birds

Evening Grosbeak

Wilson's Warbler

yellow green
upperparts

black "cap"
extends onto
forehead

♀

♂

black wings and
tail with white
wing bars

white rump and
undertail coverts

breeding

Nesting: in the fork of a deciduous tree; compact cup nest of plant fibres, grass and spider silk; pale bluish eggs are 16 x 12 mm; female incubates 4–6 eggs for about 12–14 days.

Did You Know?

These birds nest in late summer to ensure that there is a dependable source of seeds from thistles and dandelions to feed their young.

Look For

American Goldfinches delight in perching on late-summer thistle heads or poking through dandelion patches in search of seeds.

House Sparrow

Passer domesticus

A black "mask" and "bib" adorn the male of this adaptive, aggressive species. The House Sparrow's tendency to usurp territory has led to a decline in native bird populations. This sparrow will even help itself to the convenience of another bird's home, such as a bluebird or Cliff Swallow nest or a Purple Martin house. • The abundant and conspicuous House Sparrow was introduced to North America in the 1850s as part of a plan to control the insects that were damaging grain and cereal crops. As it turns out, these birds are largely vegetarian!

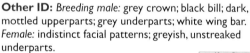

Other ID: *Breeding male:* grey crown; black bill; dark, mottled upperparts; grey underparts; white wing bar. *Female:* indistinct facial patterns; greyish, unstreaked underparts.
Size: *L* 14–17 cm; *W* 24 cm.
Voice: song is a plain, familiar *cheep-cheep-cheep-cheep;* call is a short *chill-up.*
Status: abundant year-round resident.
Habitat: townsites, urban and suburban areas, farmyards and agricultural areas, railway yards and other developed areas.

Similar Birds

Harris's Sparrow

Look For

In spring, House Sparrows feast on the buds of fruit trees. In winter, they flock together in barns in rural areas and at garbage dumps in cities.

buffy "eyebrow"

chestnut nape

light grey "cheek"

black lores and "bib"

♀

breeding

♂

Nesting: often communal; in a human-made structure, ornamental shrub or natural cavity; pair builds a large dome nest of grass, twigs and plant fibres; variably marked, white to greenish eggs are 23 x 16 mm; pair incubates 4–6 eggs for 10–13 days.

Did You Know?

The success of the House Sparrow in establishing itself in North America has to do partly with its high reproductive output. A pair may raise up to four clutches per year, with up to eight young per clutch. The House Sparrow is also a very adaptable bird, and it prefers human-modified environments, of which there is no shortage.

Glossary

accipiter: a forest hawk (genus *Accipiter*), characterized by a long tail and short, rounded wings; feeds mostly on birds.

brood: *n.* a family of young from one hatching; *v.* to incubate the eggs.

brood parasite: a bird that lays its eggs in other birds' nests.

buteo: a high-soaring hawk (genus *Buteo*), characterized by broad wings and a short, wide tail; feeds mostly on small mammals and other land animals.

cere: on birds of prey, a fleshy area at the base of the bill that contains the nostrils.

clutch: the number of eggs laid by the female at one time.

dabbling: a foraging technique used by some ducks, in which the head and neck are submerged but the body and tail remain on the water's surface; dabbling ducks can usually walk easily on land, can take off without running and have brightly coloured speculums.

"eclipse" plumage: a cryptic plumage, similar to that of females, worn by some male ducks in autumn when they moult their flight feathers and consequently are unable to fly.

flushing: when frightened birds explode into flight in response to a disturbance.

flycatching: a feeding behaviour in which the bird leaves a perch, snatches an insect in midair and returns to the same perch; also known as "hawking" or "sallying."

pelagic: refers to ocean habitat very far from land.

precocial: a bird that is relatively well developed at hatching; precocial birds usually have open eyes, extensive down and are fairly mobile.

riparian: refers to habitat along riverbanks.

sexual dimorphism: a difference in plumage, size or other characteristics between males and females of the same species.

speculum: a brightly coloured patch on the wings of many dabbling ducks.

stage: to gather in one place during migration, usually when birds are flightless or partly flightless during moulting.

stoop: a steep dive through the air, usually performed by birds of prey while foraging or during courtship displays.

crown

eyebrow/ supercilium

eye line

lore

wing bars

chin

greater coverts

throat

rump

breast

tips of primary feathers

flank

tail feathers

belly

undertail coverts

secondary feathers

Checklist

The following checklist contains 323 species of birds that are generally seen every year in Québec, New Brunswick, Prince Edward Island, Nova Scotia, or Newfoundland and Labrador. Species are grouped by family and listed in taxonomic order in accordance with the A.O.U. *Check-list of North American Birds* (7th ed.) and its supplements. An asterisk (*) identifies species that are known to nest in one or more of the provinces. A plus (+) identifies introduced species.

Waterfowl
❏ Greater White-fronted Goose
❏ Snow Goose
❏ Ross's Goose
❏ Brant
❏ Canada Goose*
❏ Mute Swan*+
❏ Wood Duck*
❏ Gadwall*
❏ Eurasian Wigeon
❏ American Wigeon*
❏ American Black Duck*
❏ Mallard*
❏ Blue-winged Teal*
❏ Northern Shoveler*
❏ Northern Pintail*
❏ Green-winged Teal*
❏ Canvasback
❏ Redhead*
❏ Ring-necked Duck*
❏ Tufted Duck
❏ Greater Scaup*
❏ Lesser Scaup
❏ King Eider
❏ Common Eider*
❏ Harlequin Duck*
❏ Surf Scoter*
❏ White-winged Scoter*
❏ Black Scoter
❏ Long-tailed Duck
❏ Bufflehead

❏ Common Goldeneye*
❏ Barrow's Goldeneye*
❏ Hooded Merganser*
❏ Common Merganser*
❏ Red-breasted Merganser*
❏ Ruddy Duck*

Grouse & Allies
❏ Chukar*+
❏ Gray Partridge*
❏ Ring-necked Pheasant*
❏ Ruffed Grouse*
❏ Spruce Grouse*
❏ Willow Ptarmigan*
❏ Rock Ptarmigan*
❏ Sharp-tailed Grouse*+

Loons
❏ Red-throated Loon*
❏ Pacific Loon
☑ Common Loon*

Grebes
❏ Pied-billed Grebe*
❏ Horned Grebe
❏ Red-necked Grebe

Petrels & Shearwaters
❏ Northern Fulmar*
❏ Cory's Shearwater
❏ Greater Shearwater
❏ Sooty Shearwater
❏ Manx Shearwater*

Storm-Petrels
- ❏ Wilson's Storm-Petrel
- ☑ Leach's Storm-Petrel

Gannets & Boobies
- ❏ Northern Gannet*

Cormorants
- ☑ Double-crested Cormorant*
- ❏ Great Cormorant*

Herons
- ❏ American Bittern*
- ❏ Least Bittern*
- ❏ Great Blue Heron*
- ❏ Great Egret
- ❏ Snowy Egret
- ❏ Little Blue Heron
- ❏ Cattle Egret
- ❏ Green Heron*
- ❏ Black-crowned Night-Heron*
- ❏ Yellow-crowned Night-Heron

Ibises
- ❏ Glossy Ibis*

Vultures
- ❏ Turkey Vulture

Kites, Hawks & Eagles
- ❏ Osprey*
- ☑ Bald Eagle*
- ❏ Northern Harrier*
- ❏ Sharp-shinned Hawk*
- ❏ Cooper's Hawk*
- ❏ Northern Goshawk*
- ❏ Red-shouldered Hawk
- ❏ Broad-winged Hawk
- ❏ Red-tailed Hawk*
- ❏ Rough-legged Hawk*
- ❏ Golden Eagle*

Falcons
- ❏ American Kestrel*
- ❏ Merlin*
- ❏ Gyrfalcon*
- ❏ Peregrine Falcon*

Rails & Coots
- ❏ Yellow Rail*
- ❏ Virginia Rail*
- ❏ Sora*

- ❏ Common Moorhen*
- ❏ American Coot*

Cranes
- ❏ Sandhill Crane

Plovers
- ❏ Northern Lapwing
- ❏ Black-bellied Plover
- ❏ Eurasian Golden-Plover
- ❏ American Golden-Plover
- ❏ Semipalmated Plover*
- ❏ Piping Plover*
- ❏ Killdeer*

Sandpipers & Allies
- ❏ Greater Yellowlegs
- ❏ Lesser Yellowlegs
- ❏ Solitary Sandpiper*
- ❏ Willet*
- ❏ Spotted Sandpiper*
- ❏ Upland Sandpiper*
- ❏ Eskimo Curlew
- ❏ Whimbrel
- ❏ Hudsonian Godwit
- ❏ Ruddy Turnstone
- ❏ Red Knot
- ❏ Sanderling
- ❏ Semipalmated Sandpiper
- ❏ Western Sandpiper
- ❏ Least Sandpiper
- ❏ White-rumped Sandpiper
- ❏ Baird's Sandpiper
- ❏ Pectoral Sandpiper
- ❏ Purple Sandpiper
- ❏ Dunlin
- ❏ Stilt Sandpiper
- ❏ Buff-breasted Sandpiper
- ❏ Short-billed Dowitcher
- ❏ Long-billed Dowitcher
- ❏ Wilson's Snipe
- ❏ American Woodcock*
- ❏ Wilson's Phalarope*
- ❏ Red-necked Phalarope*
- ❏ Red Phalarope*

Gulls & Allies
- ❏ Great Skua
- ❏ South Polar Skua
- ❏ Pomarine Jaeger

❏ Parasitic Jaeger
❏ Long-tailed Jaeger
❏ Laughing Gull*
❏ Franklin's Gull
❏ Little Gull
❏ Black-headed Gull*
❏ Bonaparte's Gull
❏ Mew Gull
❏ Ring-billed Gull*
❏ Herring Gull*
❏ Thayer's Gull
❏ Iceland Gull
❏ Lesser Black-backed Gull
❏ Glaucous Gull
✓ Great Black-backed Gull*
❏ Sabine's Gull*
❏ Black-legged Kittiwake*
❏ Ross's Gull
❏ Ivory Gull
❏ Caspian Tern*
❏ Roseate Tern*
❏ Common Tern*
❏ Arctic Tern*
❏ Forster's Tern
❏ Black Tern*

Alcids
❏ Dovekie
✓ Common Murre*
❏ Thick-billed Murre*
❏ Razorbill*
❏ Black Guillemot*
❏ Atlantic Puffin*

Pigeons & Doves
❏ Rock Pigeon*
❏ Mourning Dove*

Cuckoos
❏ Black-billed Cuckoo*
❏ Yellow-billed Cuckoo

Owls
❏ Eastern Screech-Owl*
❏ Great Horned Owl*
❏ Snowy Owl
❏ Northern Hawk Owl*
❏ Barred Owl*
❏ Long-eared Owl*
❏ Short-eared Owl*

❏ Boreal Owl*
❏ Northern Saw-whet Owl*

Nightjars
❏ Common Nighthawk*
❏ Whip-poor-will*

Swifts
❏ Chimney Swift*

Hummingbirds
❏ Ruby-throated
   Hummingbird*

Kingfishers
❏ Belted Kingfisher*

Woodpeckers
❏ Red-headed Woodpecker*
❏ Red-bellied Woodpecker
❏ Yellow-bellied Sapsucker*
❏ Downy Woodpecker*
❏ Hairy Woodpecker*
❏ American Three-toed
   Woodpecker*
❏ Black-backed Woodpecker*
❏ Northern Flicker*
❏ Pileated Woodpecker*

Flycatchers
❏ Olive-sided Flycatcher*
❏ Eastern Wood-Pewee
❏ Yellow-bellied Flycatcher*
❏ Alder Flycatcher*
❏ Willow Flycatcher*
❏ Least Flycatcher*
❏ Eastern Phoebe*
❏ Great Crested Flycatcher*
❏ Western Kingbird
❏ Eastern Kingbird*

Shrikes
❏ Loggerhead Shrike*
❏ Northern Shrike*

Vireos
❏ Blue-headed Vireo*
❏ Warbling Vireo*
❏ Philadelphia Vireo*
❏ Red-eyed Vireo*

Jays & Crows
❏ Gray Jay*
❏ Blue Jay*

❏ American Crow*
❏ Common Raven*

Larks
❏ Horned Lark*

Swallows
❏ Purple Martin*
❏ Tree Swallow*
❏ Northern Rough-winged
   Swallow*
❏ Bank Swallow*
❏ Cliff Swallow*

Chickadees and Titmice
❏ Black-capped Chickadee*
❏ Boreal Chickadee*

Nuthatches
❏ Red-breasted Nuthatch*
❏ White-breasted Nuthatch*

Creepers
❏ Brown Creeper*

Wrens
❏ Carolina Wren*
❏ House Wren*
❏ Winter Wren*
❏ Sedge Wren*
❏ Marsh Wren*

Kinglets
❏ Golden-crowned Kinglet*
❏ Ruby-crowned Kinglet*

Gnatcatchers
❏ Blue-gray Gnatcatcher*

Thrushes
❏ Northern Wheatear*
❏ Eastern Bluebird*
❏ Veery
❏ Gray-cheeked Thrush
❏ Bicknell's Thrush*
❏ Swainson's Thrush*
❏ Hermit Thrush*
❏ Wood Thrush*
❏ Fieldfare
❏ American Robin*

Mockingbirds & Thrashers
❏ Gray Catbird*

❏ Northern Mockingbird*
❏ Brown Thrasher*

Starlings
❏ European Starling*

Wagtails & Pipits
❏ American Pipit*

Waxwings
❏ Bohemian Waxwing
❏ Cedar Waxwing*

Wood-Warblers
❏ Blue-winged Warbler
❏ Tennessee Warbler*
❏ Orange-crowned Warbler*
❏ Nashville Warbler*
❏ Northern Parula*
❏ Yellow Warbler*
❏ Chestnut-sided Warbler*
❏ Magnolia Warbler*
❏ Cape May Warbler*
❏ Black-throated Blue Warbler*
❏ Yellow-rumped Warbler*
❏ Black-throated Gray Warbler
❏ Black-throated Green Warbler*
❏ Blackburnian Warbler*
❏ Pine Warbler*
❏ Prairie Warbler
❏ Palm Warbler*
❏ Bay-breasted Warbler*
❏ Blackpoll Warbler*
❏ Black-and-white Warbler*
❏ American Redstart*
❏ Ovenbird*
❏ Northern Waterthrush*
❏ Mourning Warbler*
❏ Connecticut Warbler
❏ Common Yellowthroat*
❏ Hooded Warbler
❏ Wilson's Warbler*
❏ Canada Warbler*
❏ Yellow-breasted Chat

Tanagers
❏ Summer Tanager
❏ Scarlet Tanager*

Sparrows & Allies
❏ Eastern Towhee*

❑ Cassin's Sparrow
❑ American Tree Sparrow*
❑ Chipping Sparrow*
❑ Clay-colored Sparrow*
❑ Field Sparrow*
❑ Vesper Sparrow*
❑ Lark Sparrow
❑ Savannah Sparrow*
❑ Grasshopper Sparrow
❑ Nelson's Sharp-tailed Sparrow*
❑ Fox Sparrow*
❑ Song Sparrow*
❑ Lincoln's Sparrow*
❑ Swamp Sparrow*
❑ White-throated Sparrow*
❑ White-crowned Sparrow*
❑ Dark-eyed Junco*
❑ Lapland Longspur
❑ Snow Bunting

Grosbeaks & Buntings
❑ Northern Cardinal*
❑ Rose-breasted Grosbeak*
❑ Blue Grosbeak
❑ Indigo Bunting*
❑ Dickcissel

Blackbirds & Allies
❑ Bobolink*
❑ Red-winged Blackbird*
❑ Eastern Meadowlark*
❑ Yellow-headed Blackbird
❑ Rusty Blackbird*
❑ Common Grackle*
❑ Brown-headed Cowbird*
❑ Orchard Oriole
❑ Baltimore Oriole

Finches
❑ Pine Grosbeak*
❑ Purple Finch*
❑ House Finch*
❑ Red Crossbill*
❑ White-winged Crossbill*
❑ Common Redpoll*
❑ Hoary Redpoll
❑ Pine Siskin*
❑ American Goldfinch*
❑ Evening Grosbeak*

Old World Sparrows
❑ House Sparrow*

Select References

American Ornithologists' Union. 1998. *Check-list of North American Birds.* 7th ed. (and its supplements). American Ornithologists' Union, Washington, D.C.

Burrows, Roger. 2002. *Birds of Atlantic Canada.* Lone Pine Publishing, Edmonton, Alberta.

Elphick, C., J. B. Dunning, Jr., and D.A. Sibley, eds. 2001. *National Audubon Society The Sibley Guide to Bird Life & Behavior.* Alfred A. Knopf, New York.

Roth, Sally. 1998. *Attracting Birds to Your Backyard: 536 Ways to Turn Your Yard and Garden into a Haven for Your Favorite Birds.* Rodale Press, Inc. Emmaus, Pennsylvania.

Sibley, D. A. 2000. *National Audubon Society: The Sibley Guide to Birds.* Alfred A. Knopf, New York.

Index

Belted Kingfisher